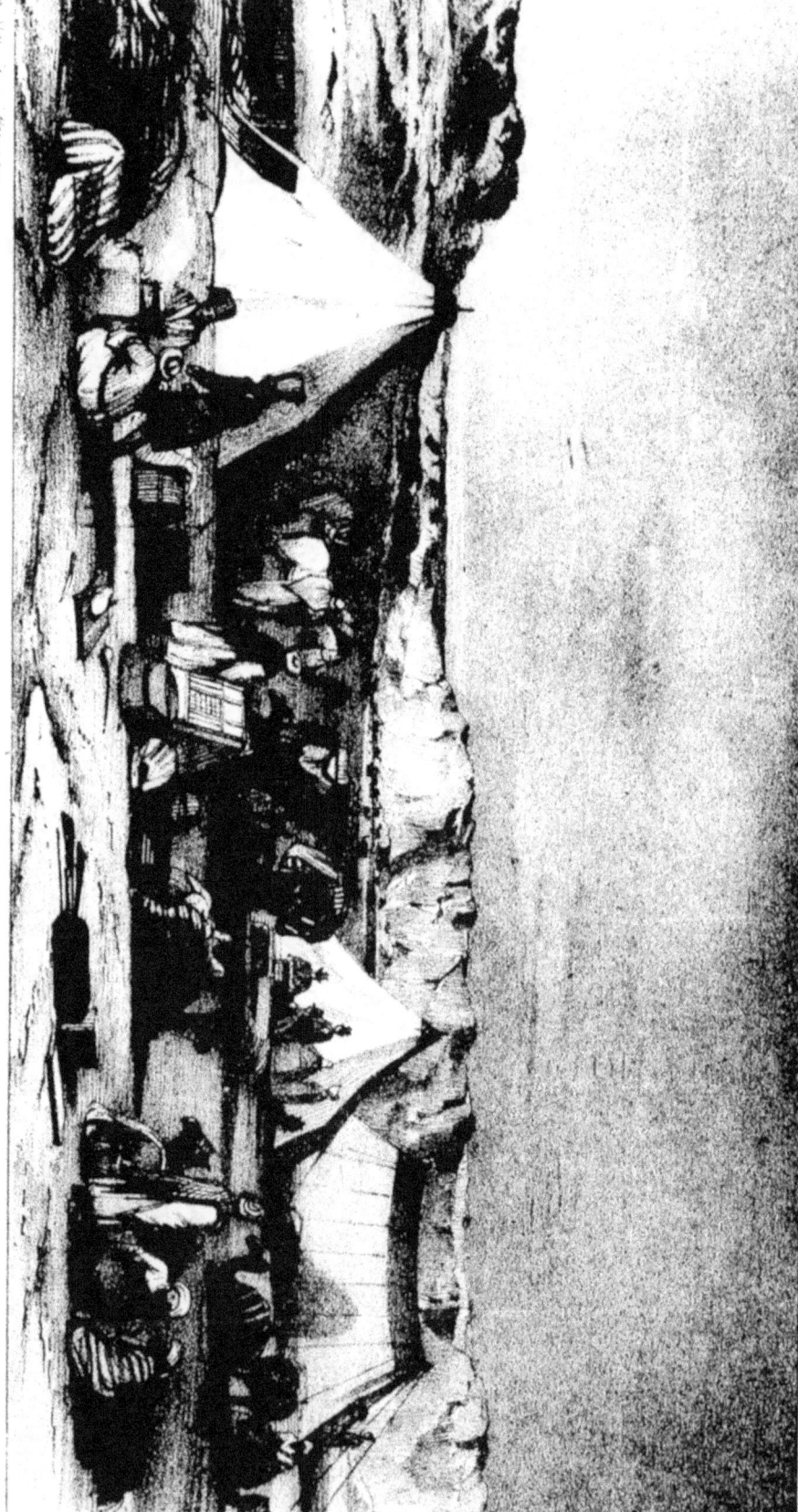

THE DRUNKARD

London Published by Henry Coburn, 18, Mh Road, 8. 1 1841

DIARY

OF

A TOUR

IN

GREECE, TURKEY, EGYPT,

AND

THE HOLY LAND.

BY

THE HON. MRS. G. L. DAWSON DAMER.

IN TWO VOLUMES.

VOL II.

LONDON:

HENRY COLBURN, PUBLISHER,

GREAT MARLBOROUGH STREET.

1841.

CONTENTS

OF

THE SECOND VOLUME.

CHAPTER VII.

CHAPTER VIII.

CHAPTER IX.

CHAPTER X.

CHAPTER XI.

CHAPTER XII.

CHAPTER XIII.

CHAPTER XIV.

APPENDIX I.

APPENDIX II.

APPENDIX III.

APPENDIX IV.

DIARY.

CHAPTER I.

Pilgrimage to Bethlehem—An Arab funeral—The Wilderness—The grotto—David's tomb—Prince Pückler Muskau — Jewish masonry — Pool of Bethesda—Armenian convent—Bazaar of Jerusalem—A disagreeable mistake.

DECEMBER 4TH.—We were nearly deterred from our pilgrimage to Bethlehem, by the account of the dust and wind; but fearing that at this season the weather was not likely to improve, we set off in a perfect whirlwind, and the fine dust so blinded us, that Minney and I resigned ourselves, *tête baissée*, to a little black slave's guidance. After an hour and a half's actually painful ride through a black valley, and over a cold mountain, we arrived at a monument distinguished as Rachel's tomb.

The spot is, I believe, correctly chosen as the place of her interment, but the building itself does not appear of an ancient construction. An Arab funeral was taking place close to it, attended by about fifty wild and starved-looking Arabs. The only ceremonial appeared to consist in each individual contributing a stone towards raising a mound, which had gained considerable elevation when we passed it a few hours afterwards, on our return from Bethlehem.

There was a wild, ferocious expression of countenance prevailing among these Arabs, that we had never before been so much struck by; the very whiteness of their teeth and shape of their mouths gave them a false and savage appearance. One would most unwillingly have met them in a less frequented path.

We left Bethlehem on our left, for the purpose of visiting the Pools of Solomon, and passed a fountain which our attendants pointed out as the spot where the shepherds first heard " the tidings of great joy." There was everything in the position and the neighbouring pasturage to favour the impression, and I look back to it with much more conviction than any I received subsequently, on being shewn the spot where the Saviour was born, and the magi adored.

The pools are situated in a valley, surrounded on all sides by a desolate rocky country. They are only three in number, and of immense size, in perfect repair, and are undoubtedly the work of Solomon, for the conduit still exists, which to this day supplies the mosque of Omar with water. The pools are fed by considerable springs a few hundred yards from the upper one.

Commanding the pass is a Turkish castle,
flanked by four towers for their protection.
This precaution was necessary in a country
which, besides the innumerable wars it has
had to encounter with its foreign enemies,
has been at all times torn by civil discord
and petty warfare.

Within ten years Bethlehem has been at
war with Jerusalem ; hostilities, jealousies,
and hatred lasted six years, and impeded all
communications to such a degree that travellers were compelled to be protected by
the Arabs of one town during their progress
to the other, and were thus handed on in
their journey through hostile bands. "The
abomination of desolation" is depictcd at
every step.

On leaving these wells or pools for Bethlehem, the aqueduct runs along the path
you ride on, and here and there the ruins of
villages are perceived, and a few green
patches, produced by the water escaping

from the reservoir and acting refreshingly upon the thirsty land. Bethlehem looks as you approach it on this side much more like a fortress than a convent. It is surrounded by a good deal of cultivation, and much remains of the planted terraces of olives and vineyards; the latter have in almost all instances a large round tower, from which there is a watch to protect them, and these at a distance look like Martello towers.

Bethlehem is on an acclivity, and the road very difficult and unsafe to surmount. Had the wind been less cutting, we should have made a still further *détour* to what is called the Desert of St. John; which I imagined must be the *Wilderness*, till reminded that it was beyond Jordan. It is by tradition the birth-place of St. John the Baptist; but this is not corroborated by the mention or remains of any considerable town in that always desert tract of country; and as all the great dignitaries of the Jewish

church were at that period *priests* of a *city*,
Zachariah must have dwelt in one, and that
of Hebron is the locality that more distinctly points itself out ; and there a tree is
shewn as that under which Abraham leant
when he entertained the strangers (angels.)

The general desertion from this neighbourhood is very decided, and within a few
years the increase of jackals, wild boars,
&c. &c., so great, that they venture to the
very precincts of Jerusalem.   A Jew with
whom Mr. Young lodged at Hebron, shewed
him papers, from which he could trace his
forefathers for six hundred years, and their
property in Hebron ; and he told Mr. Y.
that in his grandfather's time between sixty
and seventy villages had appertained to this
district, and at this moment not more than
fifty could be pointed out.   But to return to
our visiting Bethlehem.

The effect of approaching a fortification
so little corresponded with the idea one had
formed of the lowly state of Bethlehem, that

it required the very long time we were kept waiting for admittance to re-settle our impressions. We had passed through a fine court, supported by twenty-four pillars of (apparently) stained red lime-stone, which in this country is of so fine a grain as almost to approach the quality of marble. At a very low door a lay-brother knocked without the slightest result, the wind being so high that our tapping did not reach the Franciscan's ears. At last, some stones thrown at a small window produced more effect, and we were shewn into the refectory, and hospitably received by a Spanish monk, who seemed much disappointed at finding we neither intended dining nor lodging at the convent. Our progress in riding had been so tedious, that we hardly ventured to drink the excellent coffee brought us, for fear our time would be too short to visit the Grotto of the Nativity, and enable us to get back to Jerusalem before the gates were closed.

The grotto, like the holy sepulchre, is spoiled by a profusion of ornament ; and the Latins, Greeks, and Armenians, here, as elsewhere, share in the possession of the sacred places : the Latins here, however, have the advantage in having possession of the place of nativity—the stable and the manger ; the Greeks that of the manifestation ; and a painted representation of the magi distinguishes the spot, with a star above. Silver lamps adorn the altars in great profusion and richness, and many are late presents of the Queen of the French and the Emperor of Russia.

The tombs of St. Jerome, St. Eusebius, and two female Roman saints, of the family of Spina Gracchi, occupy niches in this part of the building. Above the spot which the manger was supposed to occupy, the natural form of the rocks is seen, and encourages one to rely on the identity of ground selected by the piety of the Empress

Helena, whose memory must be revered, as she was the instrument of commemorating and preserving the sites of all the most sacred and interesting Christian associations; for if she were misled occasionally in her pious researches, yet she formed the most important and earliest link to the chain of local evidence, and her works throughout the Holy Land remain in a very general state of preservation.

The name of Bethlehem, or Ephrata, signifying House of Bread, was said to have been given first by Abraham; it is next distinguished as the birth-place of David, and where he tended the flocks of Jesse. Great tracts of pasturage can be traced in the immediate neighbourhood of Bethlehem; the valley adjoining is believed to be the scene of the story of Ruth.

After making extensive purchases in rosaries and carved mother-of-pearl, on which the great industry of the community

of Bethlehem is employed, we returned by
a shorter road, skirting the hill that conducted to the Pool of Siloam ; and the wind
having abated, our ride was much less of a
penance than that we had experienced from
Jerusalem.

DECEMBER 5TH.—Mr. and Mrs. Nicholaison and their little daughter paid us a
visit. The latter, an intelligent girl of nine,
gave Minney an excellent Arabic lesson of
familiar phrases, which she has offered to
follow up. We called on Mr. Young to
look at a *Tartahuan* or *Sad-hakief*, a sort
of double palanquin, or cages, to be placed
on each side of a camel, for our approaching journey. I am already compassionating
the poor animal that is to have Minney and
myself inclosed in these wooden residences.

We then proceeded with Mr. Y. and his
intelligent old Jewish dragoman, Joseph, to
visit David's tomb, situated near the gate of
the same name, and inclosed by a mosque.

With a permission from the governor, Christians were allowed to descend into the vaulted portion of the building; but now we were only permitted to look down from the middle of the flight of steps.

Prince Pückler Muskau, we were told, has been the cause of this exclusion, (as also in the instance of visiting the Mosque of Omar,) by making a forcible entrance without permission beyond where the general firman entitled him to go. The *custode's* opposition continuing, Prince Pückler drew his sword, and threatened to cut down any one who obstructed his passage. The great object of enforcing the privileges of the firman was to avoid paying the smallest fee; at Jaffa, when he had taken a bath, he presented the said firman as an excuse for not liquidating his debt of three piastres (1s. 3d. of our money). This seems to have incurred the wrath of the Jews, Christians, and Infidels. Consuls, governors, and guides,

have all some cause of complaint. I am
curious to see his own version of his journeying and *succès en Orient*.

The strictest order has, since this *esclandre*,
been given against any but Mussulmen
being admitted into the tomb. Sir Moses
Montefiore, the only exception, (whom the
governor and Mr. Nicholaison accompanied,) remained for some time in prayer,
reading some of the Psalms in Hebrew with
his interpreter, Mr. Levi, who afterwards
translated them into English for the benefit
of Sir Moses and Lady Montefiore. After
the tomb of the Prophet, that of David is
the highest in veneration with the Mahometans.

After a very long, and wet walk round
the walls, which, from rain and the accumulation of rubbish, made our progress
very difficult, we arrived at a most interesting spot, which I think has not been particularly remarked by travellers, and was

first pointed out by Mr. Y. to Sir Andrew Bernard. It is evidently the spring of a magnificent arch, which must have afforded the communication between the Mount Zion and Moriah, thus connecting the Temple with Mount Zion, and crossing the Valley commonly called that of the Cheese-mongers.

The span of the arch must have been at least sixty feet, and have rivalled in beauty and magnificence the still existing and adjoining wall from which it springs. It was nearly one hundred feet high, above, perhaps, an equal depth of rubbish collected at its base: the first layer of stone consists of magnificent masses, hewn out with great care, and George thought as large as any Cyclopean remains he had seen at Mycene and the Grecian colonies in Italy, only that instead of rude blocks these were beautifully hewn and channelled in the form which is supposed to distinguish the

works of Solomon ; over this again the wall
is built in an equally regular manner, but
with less solidity and grandeur, and resembling the construction of the Colosseum.
This again is crowned by what reminds me
of the rustic architecture to be seen in
the substructure of some of the palaces at
Florence.

The superior character of the Jewish
masonry is very striking : some of the
blocks were thirty feet by seven, perfectly
unornamented but by a sharp indented line,
looking as freshly cut as if they had just
been laid, and this after nearly 3000 years !
So striking is the fulfilment of the prophecies, " that the worst of heathen should
possess the land ; that the holy places
should be defiled." " I will pour down the
stones thereof into the valley ; and I will
discover the foundations thereof."

It is at this, the S. E. and most perfectly
preserved angle of the foundations of the

Temple, that some of the most devout of the Jews assemble on Fridays after midday, when their Sabbath begins. They are to be seen kneeling on the original stone, with tears of penitence rolling down their cheeks, and in the posture of humiliation, and deprecating in scriptural language the wrath of the Almighty, and praying for their restoration, and a renewal of his mercies.

We then proceeded through rubbish and dirt of every kind, having unluckily chosen our road through the receptacle for dead horses, &c., for the purpose of seeing the Pool of Bethesda : it is close to St. Stephen's gate, (and spot of Lapidation), and is a large reservoir, but now without water. There is great doubt entertained of its identity ; its vicinity to the Temple, and what is considered to have been the Sheep Market, affords the only ground of probability.

We next visited an Armenian convent,

built on the site of the house of Caiphas ; a
deserted Christian church is in this vicinity,
built near the site of the house alleged to
have been that of the birth-place of the
Virgin. It is in such good preservation
that one felt inclined to wish that the
edifice had been obtained and converted
into the Protestant church, as the spot of
ground obtained for that purpose has little
chance of answering the intention, owing to
the absence of labourers ; the foundation
itself, begun to be dug a year ago, is not
yet completed.

Our way home lay through the *Via Dolo-
rosa*, and the alternate changes of the
weather from rain to sunshine gave a very
picturesque effect of shadow to the old
vaulted passages and flights of steps in
which Jerusalem abounds ; the streets are
dirty, dull, and ill-paved. Sometimes the
archways would furnish beautiful studies for
an artist.

The bazaars are narrow, bad, and ill-furnished : we could obtain neither cup, plate, nor dish of any kind to add to our canteen; and for knives, were obliged to substitute the common dagger of the country. No meat of any kind but mutton and goat's flesh, can be had; beef seems to be unknown, and vegetables so scarce that a cauliflower made quite an epoch in our kitchen, and for potatoes we substituted rice, which is the grand and indeed chief sustenance of the people. Although at only thirty miles from the sea-coast, fish is never brought to Jerusalem, and consequently indifferent poultry and mutton are the only food for European consumption, eggs being scarce, and butter *nil*. No pudding or pastry of any kind is to be thought of, and one is quite surprised how soon one becomes reconciled to so limited a bill of fare.

The clay vessels for drawing water are the

only ones used for drinking, and for eating purposes, a platter for the rice *pillau*, of which all the family partake. Coarse and ill-baked bread forms the sole nourishment of the majority of the Syrian and Arab population ; and I believe a cup, glass, or plate, would not be met with in any Mahometan residence throughout the country, unless in that of some Turkish *employé*.

The town is full of beggars, cripples, and lepers, but the stirring population is vastly mixed, and interesting to behold : Arabs, Bedouins, armed to the teeth, and admirably mounted, are frequently met, and in the governor's yard we saw more than a hundred wild-looking men, who, we were told, served as a sort of irregular cavalry to the Pacha.

Sometimes the general stillness of the town is interrupted by a cavalier rushing by you at full speed, waving his *djereed* with great dexterity and grace, and answering the description of the mode of attack of the infidels at the time of the Paladins.

Over St. Stephen's gate are some coarse ornaments, resembling lions and rosaces : as any resemblance of living things is forbidden to the Mahometans, may not these almost effaced ornaments be of the time of the crusades? We persuaded Mr. and Mrs. Young to come home with us, and try our convent fare, which really, under Denino's auspices, was improving daily ; and Mrs. Y. having sent for some soup plates, afforded us a perfect fête.

The accessories of our convent furniture consisted of mattresses, six chairs, and two tables ; but with our Smyrna purchases of carpets and counterpanes, and our dear Dover chairs, our rooms were, for Jerusalem, sumptuously furnished. Our canteen, containing only two tea-cups, obliges us to breakfast *à trois reprises*, and we cannot often change our plates ; but constant exercise and excitement make us overlook every deficiency, and we very much appreciate our *portable* comforts, although on this occasion we ran great risk of an original quality in our portable soup, as, among our medical provisions, we had brought a large lump of a preparation for blisters, and this was inclosed in tin, without a label.

Christine, in her anxiety to have soup *at hand*, for which she mistook this, transferred the *stock* from the *panier de médecine*, to that of the *provision de bouche*. I wish truth would allow me to go a little further into the detail of Denino seasoning our dreadful potage, but it was found out in time. Our doctor shuddered at the notion of the probable distressing results which would have attended our swallowing a spoonful of such a mixture, and took this opportunity of renewing his warnings, " *Madame devoit éviter des condimens trop héroiques.*"

CHAPTER II.

Village of Bethany—Tomb of Lazarus—View of the
Dead Sea—Accounts of Acre—Termination of
the Rhamazan—Our Doctor in great request—
Want of medical attendance — The Burying
Ground—Visit to Mount Calvary—Glorious sun-
set—Laziness of the Jews—Leave Jerusalem.

DECEMBER 6TH.—Owing to its being the
Mahometan sabbath, we could not set off
on our ride to Bethany till after one, when
the gates would be open. We crossed the
Valley of Jehosaphat, and proceeded to
Bethany, leaving Siloam on our right. In
Scripture, the distance is said to be a sab-
bath's journey, (not quite two miles,) but

the road is so steep and rugged, our ride must have occupied one hour and a half.

This village, like all in the vicinity of Jerusalem, is in the most ruined and miserable state; groups of ill-clothed, or rather, hardly clothed, peasants, were lying in idleness among the ruins, and appearing indifferent to the spots they chose, as some, who might have selected a less bleak and exposed situation, were sitting on the roofs of their stone habitations, or holes cut in the rocks. In the centre of the village you are shewn the tomb of Lazarus, and you descend a flight of eighteen steps, to the place of his interment, which is capacious enough to allow your *creeping* in. This narrow descent does not answer to one's impression of the place from whence our Saviour called to Lazarus to come forth.

About a hundred yards further, a cavern in a rock presented itself, which answered much more to our preconceived ideas, as

one large stone might have closed it, and
"have been rolled away," and a space sur-
rounds it, where "the much people who
followed" might have stood spectators to
the miracle. Our convent guide advised our
going a little further, to shew us the stone
upon which our Saviour was said to have
been sitting when Mary conveyed to him
the news of her brother's death.

The ruins of Bethphage are discernible,
and we were surprised at our cicerone fur-
nishing us with no tradition of the house of
Martha and Mary, or that of Simon the
leper, where our Saviour was anointed with
spikenard.

In returning, by the Mount of Olives, we
had again a favourable evening for the view
of the Dead Sea, and the spot to which
Israel was led by Joshua, and the general
view was more distinct from this point than
from the higher position. We could not
pass the Chapel of the Ascension without
again visiting it, as well as the Garden of

Gethsemane. Nothing appears to me so certain as the identity of this sacred spot, and of a portion of rock, now of a perfectly smooth, though not level, surface, upon which our Saviour is said to have knelt and fell; every portion of this garden (as it is called) so describes the awful and touching features of the scene. We succeeded in sawing off a large piece of wood from the oldest olive-tree; and I hope we escaped observation, in setting so bad an example for pious thefts.

It is only by repeatedly visiting the immediate country about Jerusalem that one becomes aware of the magnificent scale of its hills and valleys : however desolate, arid, and uncultivated, there is an air of majesty about them to which no description can do justice. The Valley of Judgment cannot bear its name, without inspiring almost thrilling feelings at its depth and vastness; the stony barrenness of the soil at this season meets with no relief, but we are told, that the luxuriance and beauty of the spring flowers cause all this to disappear, and that the neighbourhood of Jerusalem becomes, in April and May, one vast and fragrant flower-garden.

On our return to the convent we found Joseph, the Consul's dragoman, who brought us very unfavourable accounts of the neighbourhood of Acre, and proved to us the impracticability of our going by Damascus; some English travellers, to whom the Governor of Acre did not feel justified in affording protection by land to Beyrout, having been obliged to hire a native vessel and proceed by sea; and we fear we must now turn our minds and our caravans in the direction of Gaza, on our way to Cairo. This change of plan disappoints us much as to our Balbec prospects; perhaps our arriving earlier in Egypt may enable us to realize our wish of visiting Thebes.

The old Jew had brought his wife, Sarah,

and his pretty little girl, Rachel, to see us :
they only spoke Spanish, and were magnifi-
cently dressed ; and the mother, in age and
costume, might have afforded the model for
the Rebecca of Ivanhoe. She is Joseph's
fourth wife, and might be his great-grand-
daughter ; but the family group would have
been a beautiful one, to draw, their dresses
and cast of features were so exactly those
chosen by the old masters in their representations of patriarchs and their families.

DECEMBER 7TH.— We were disturbed
from our sleep by a regular cannonade, and
my first idea was, that Jerusalem was in a
state of siege ; but it turned out the very
common-place event of some guns firing on
the ushering in of the Beiram, and the re-
joicing attending the termination of the
Rhamazan. I partook of it, as it is quite
distressing to have one's horse led by atte-
nuated Arabs, and feel that all they are
watching is the setting sun, at the very

moment we wish the light prolonged, so as not to be shut out of the gates.

We had been trying to engage an Arab, much recommended by Sir A. Bernard, whom Mr. Y. could not succeed in finding, as he was always from home ; this morning, our pilgrim, or rather seller of rosaries, offered himself as a guide, which offer met with no encouragement. M. Chacaton hinted to us that he was a tailor by trade, who had undertaken to put his wardrobe in repair ; our turbaned friend, however, insisted, in bad Italian, on his qualifications for a travelling servant, and at last we discovered that the same individual pursued these various avocations, and that the very man with whom we had for days been endeavouring to obtain an interview, was the same whom George and always been trying to eject from our convent quarters.

Just as I was setting off with our doctor, to see the fête of Beiram outside the walls,

he was summoned to the governor's, to
attend one of the officers. He has visited
at least forty patients a day since our
arrival, and been consulted daily by more
than double that number, and we are followed from our convent by the poor, asking
to see our *hakim*. We do not cease being
grateful that we took the resolution of
bringing him with us, so great a comfort and
relief has he proved in this wretched place,
where, in a population of fifteen thousand,
there has only been one medical attendant,
a German convert, whom we found at the
point of death, without any assistant to com-
pound or to dispense the scanty stock of
medicine he possessed.

The doctor says he has seen two people
who have recovered from the plague ; one
an old man who is left paralytic, another a
youth who is left dumb. He supposes that
the virus of the disease entered the system,
and thus left behind the proofs of its venom.

Many Jews have consulted him; and it is sad to know the vast proportion of sickness solely caused by famine and cold,—the general disease being low fever, which can only be relieved by better living. We made up small packets of quinine to distribute, which were eagerly accepted; and the doctor dispensed occasionally soup, bread, and biscuit, and some article of warm coarse clothing among his patients; these were more gratefully received than money, which forms a great contrast to our English poor.

One cannot help wishing to suggest that some of the funds subscribed for the Jewish Society, should be applied to establishing a physician, and a regular supply of medical assistance. Might it not be feasible, under proper and judicious management, to afford the poor of Jerusalem, on the plan practised in England, some relief by soup tickets, or rather bread tickets, in a country where the grain is abundant, and the climate allows such food to be of sufficient nourishment to its inhabitants, many of whom I have actually seen during our rides eat grass and clover? The attention to their physical sufferings might lead to higher results, and put our missionaries, and those desirous of conveying religious instruction, in more direct and intimate communication with Jew and Gentile.

Have we not the Divine example in more than one instance, of the sick being cured, the lepers cleansed, and the hungry fed, before religious instruction was imparted? I feel convinced that greater charity could not be exercised at Jerusalem than by the appointment of medical attendance; the selection should fall on some one whose zeal would induce him to bear the sacrifice of settling in such a country. Devotion to the cause is more required than great skill, as the prevailing maladies are obviously low fever and ophthalmia, for both of which the remedies are well understood.

Minney and her father during this time rode to see the Prophets' Tombs, into which they could not effect an entrance. They described the monument as having little claim to its appellation, as its architecture is comparatively of a recent period, and evidently not Jewish. The doors are of solid stone, and it is supposed could not have been hung after the building was terminated, but at the time of its construction; the ornamental part of the frieze was in very delicate and beautiful work, and in a degree of preservation very superior to its general state.

We then proceeded outside the walls to the burying-grounds, which presented a very pretty scene, as the Turkish women were celebrating the first day of the *Beiram*, in visiting the tombs of their friends, and ornamenting them with fresh flowers. Some had placed tents, where they were eating and amusing themselves ; several groups made signs to us to go and join them.

Our European dresses seemed to cause them more interest and amusement than the Turkish women had shewn at Constantinople. I tried to attract some very pretty little children, employing my little stock of Arabic in calling out *Imshi*, which did not produce the desired effect, and even disturbed the gravity of our Cavasse Hassan. It seems that I had substituted the *va via*, for *vienni qui*.

A poor little Arab girl was among a group of well-dressed children, with nothing on but a sort of blouse of coarse canvas, but was a complete miniature of the Arabian style of countenance—such a clear olive complexion, long cut eye, a beautifully-formed mouth, and rather dilated nostrils. I gave her a little piece of money, which was received with much pleasure and surprise. On walking on, I soon heard a great wrangle raised by the Turkish children, imitating their elders, in despoiling this poor little Arab. My *Frank* interference however speedily settled the matter, and the little Turks looked so crest-fallen, that I hope this may be *de bonne augure* for the future settlement of the question.

I finished my day by paying Mrs. Young a visit, where I acted as newspaper, in telling them what was, in fact, rather old political gossip, which their long failure of Galignanis had made them miss. We went home very heavy at heart at finding no letters from Alexandria.

DECEMBER 8TH.—We went to church at the Consul's, and our congregation amounted to only ten, including an American missionary and two German converts. The consciousness that we were attending Divine worship at Jerusalem made the service particularly impressive; and the text, taken from the lesson of the day, Luke xxi., " And there shall be signs in the sun, and in the moon, and in the stars, and upon the whole earth distress of nations with perplexity," was very ably treated by Mr. Nicholaison, and appeared a most forcible anticipation of what every day becomes more apparent here, some great and general change.

Just as we got back to our convent door, Mr. Young overtook us, to tell us of a fresh revolt at Mount Hebron ; four hundred men having been sent for by the governor, to reinforce the eleven hundred who had gone two days before to put down a less serious disturbance. As fast as one rebellion is quelled here, another springs up ; and the soldiers are so little to be relied on that the governor's son, though willing to give us an escort to conduct us beyond Mount Hebron, strongly advised our making the *détour* of Ramla and Gaza, where the country is (for Syria) in a secure state.

In the afternoon we again visited Mount Calvary; the organ was playing, but anything less impressive it is difficult to conceive: the overture to Lodoaiska was one of the pieces selected. The sacred spots we wished once more to see, were pointed out in so irreverent a manner that it caused an almost painful impression; the closeness and the accumulation of bad smells at that part of the church which adjoins the Holy Sepulchre was something dreadful. We saw the Pillar of the Flagellation, which we had missed on our first visit, and which has all the appearance of an ancient column.

It is satisfactory, with regard to the site of Mount Calvary, to observe, as was pointed out to us by Mr. Young, that the stones composing the walls of the town in this direction have all the character of Roman construction, and a complete absence of the larger blocks that distinguished the Jewish substructures in other directions of the

walls, so that it encourages one to believe
the original walls were within those of this
quarter, and would at once establish the fact
of Mount Calvary being outside the city at
our Saviour's crucifixion. That the site of
Pilate's house is correctly fixed, there appears
no doubt; at present it is occupied by a
Turkish barrack. We then walked out by
St. Stephen's gate, and looked up at the
spot allotted to Mahomet at the day of
doom; we had intended to reach the Garden
of Gethsemane, but the day closed too suddenly to allow our doing so, though the
distance was only computed at a Sabbath-
day's journey (six furlongs).

I never saw so glorious a sunset; the
clouds of purple were of the most vivid and
beautiful tints; any attempt to represent
them in painting would have appeared exaggerated: it must have been such a sky as
this which our Saviour pointed out as the
one from which the Pharisee could deduce

an opinion of the future weather: " Ye hypocrites, ye can discern the face of the sky, but ye cannot discern the signs of the times." George went with Mr. Y. to the house of the Governor, whose son received them with great civility, but confirmed the bad news we had heard from Hebron.

We met two very beautifully accoutred officers coming to our convent, in search of the hakim, to afford *military* assistance, their colonel having been taken suddenly ill. Our mild-looking Christian servant, Youssoff, came to ask us for a horse and a new set of clothes, preparatory to our journey into the desert; he also signified that his services were to be confined to leading my horse or dromedary when the occasion required, and attending only on me. These demands and conditions not suiting our arrangements, I was grieved to see Youssoff's steps turned towards Jaffa.

DECEMBER 9TH.—We were again disappointed about our letters, and the Consul did not seem surprised, as it is supposed that the Egyptian and Turkish Governments frequently detain letters of any bulk directed to foreigners, lest they should transmit some political information; perhaps we are spared some bad news, which might make our journey through the Desert one of tedious anxiety. We employed all the morning in writing to England, and only went out to dine at Mr. Young's, where the *appareil* of an English dinner afforded a great contrast to our convent scramble.

DECEMBER 10TH.—The wrangling of our horse purveyors made our departure appear impracticable; but after George had shewn great determination of resisting Jewish and Mussulman extortion, we succeeded in getting the Tartahuan out of the maker's hands, and proceeded to pay Mrs. Nicholaison a farewell visit.

Some interesting conversation was in-

terrupted by the entrance of a German
Jew, whom Mrs. N. described as one of
their few converts, and one whom they had
prevailed upon to exercise himself in the
shoe-making trade, as extreme and hope-
less idleness was the great evil they had to
contend against. In this instance their
good intentions had sadly failed; for the
good Isaac, with many apologies, produced
a child's shoe from his pocket he had been
for some months manufacturing for Mrs.
N.'s little girl, and expressed great regret
at the utter impossibility of making its fel-
low till the mildness of the weather allowed
him to work; for he said that at present
his fingers and faculties were equally benumbed. This declaration was as seriously
made as it was absurdly delivered. The
complaints of being unemployed were very
general, but every attempt to encourage industry had failed, even with regard to those
in the greatest state of destitution.

One of the Spanish Jews had shewn some talent for sculpture, in making a pretty candlestick from the sandstone of the country. Mr. Y. bespoke its *pendant* and a vase for the centre ornament; but on being sent home, the vase proved quite crooked, and the candlestick out of all proportion with the original: in short, the stimulus of gain is not yet sufficient to arouse their moral or physical energies, though " to beg they are *not* ashamed."

We actually left Jerusalem at half-past two; our last view of Mount Olivet was from the leads of the convent, and we left our artist to take the view of that unpicturesque but most interesting spot, the Garden of Gethsemane. Mr. and Mrs. Young accompanied us on our road as far as the village, or rather to the site of the ancient Emmaus.

We reached our *gîte* at Aber-Gosh about sunset, expecting to find the sheik's house

" swept and garnished" for our reception ; but great was our dismay when Denino met us with a chicken half-plucked in his hand, and told us that the sheik's house was shut up, and that there was only one room for our whole party, *à la maison d'un individu*, and that the sheik was himself absent ; of this fact we were well aware, as he was the famous robber whom the government had so long failed in capturing, and who had for many years levied a tax on passing travellers, but his son was allowed the privilege of exercising hospitality ; and after some *démêlé*, we succeeded in getting possession of a room without a single article of furniture.

Unluckily for us, the horse loaded with our folding chairs had fallen, and so ingeniously as to render all unfit for use, so that we had to sit on our saddles round our table, which was composed of a packing-case. But all these contrivances added to our amusement and appetite; and how our good dinner was produced was incomprehensible, unless by a *coup de baguette.*

On leaving Jerusalem, one was impressed with a feeling of awe, in passing by the valley of Jehoshaphat, associated as it appears with the denunciations contained in the prophecies of Joel; and it made one ask oneself, under what awful circumstances we might next contemplate this spot?

The only exception to the generally melancholy expression of countenance of the inhabitants of Jerusalem, was that of one of our guides, who was deaf and dumb; he was always bursting with good humour and wild animal spirits, and his pantomimic manner was quite successful in expressing to us whatever he wished: in short, it served us much better than Arabic.

CHAPTER III.

Our deaf and dumb guide—The country about Jerusalem—Ramla—Arrival at the Latin convent—
Illness of the superior—A sociable monk—Delightful garden—Esdoud—One of Mehemet Ali's
messengers—Uncomfortable quarters, and trouble-
some visitors—Dummy's good qualities—Splendid
appearance of the sky—Our lodgings at Gaza—
The inspector of quarantine, and his adventures.

DECEMBER 11TH.—We reposed in great
safety in the robber's house, and we might
have been *aux reprèsailles* with him, as all
the goods and wearing apparel were left
scattered and unprotected. In the confusion of departure, I was quite afraid lest
we should carry off our neighbour's goods.

Dummy constituted himself my chevalier, pointing out the resort of wild boar and gazelle in the most ingenious manner, assuming by turns the *allure* of these animals, and making his ungainly person almost graceful in personating the latter animal. There was soon an opportunity of judging of the merit of his pantomime, in the shape of three pretty gazelles close to our path; I was very glad that our *padrone cacciatore* was too far beyond us to try his gun.

The agreeable but threatening weather at last declared itself in a heavy shower; and poor Minney, on unfurling her umbrella, so frightened her horse that he started, and threw her upon her face. She fortunately escaped with a scratched nose and chin, and very bravely called out she was not hurt.

Our poor Dummy touched me much as soon as he saw she was not hurt: he looked

earnestly at me, and then pointed towards
Heaven, as if to direct my gratitude thither.
As Syria is not likely to have produced an
Abbé de l'Epée, this poor man's sense of
religion must have been innate, and its
impression was the more pure and remarkable ; no Christian of our party would
have thus immediately referred to a superintending Providence. I had observed it
on another occasion : on dividing some
bread with him, he first kissed it, and
looked upwards most devoutly. Minney's
little accident made the rest of our journey
less lively.

We found Denino installed at the Latin
convent, to which our Jerusalem community had begged us to go, instead of to
our former quarters at the Greek convent.
We had been told by some monks, who had
passed us on the road coming from Cairo,
that we had been expected at Ramla the
night before. We had hardly got off our

horses before our doctor was summoned to visit the superior, and our, or rather the *hakim's* arrival, was of most fortunate occurrence, as he found the reverend *Padre* suffering under a violent attack of brain fever, of the character of which the monks were so entirely ignorant, that they were sitting round his bed laughing at the incoherencies and ravings of his delirium : luckily, our provision for blisters had not been all converted into soup, but there were no means of making a plaster, till I devoted a glove for the purpose ; no stock of medicine of any kind was to be found in the convent.

The approach to Ramla, from Jerusalem, is much more favourable to its appearance than from Jaffa ; the mixture of olive, cactus, pomegranate, and fig-trees, occasionally dotted by palm trees, had such a pretty effect among ruined mosques, illuminated by the setting sun. All nature seemed

refreshed by the late rain, and the bright-
ness of the vegetation formed a striking
contrast to the aridity of the country about
Jerusalem, which, at this season, is without
a blade of grass, and the soil is as closely
overlaid with flints as the environs of
Brighton; however, all this is said to disappear in the early spring, and the green
corn, and abundance of flowers, are described
as making the country appear a perfect
garden; there is a fearful report of a *cordon
sanitaire* making Al Arish, one of our next
points, impassable; and we are now in all
the anxiety of trying to ascertain the safest
direction for our journey.

We of womankind are entirely separated
from the rest of the convent, and not even
allowed to cross the court. I suppose we
ought to be flattered at being considered so
dangerous; a fat, merry old Spaniard, however, trusts himself with us in an unflatter-
ing manner, very anxious to restore our

energies with *Rosoglio*, particularly those of *La poveretta stracciata*, as Minney is described with her scratched face.

The doctor's remedies have already proved efficacious for the superior, as, after six days and nights *insomnie*, the poor sufferer has had an hour's sleep, to-morrow being the seventh day, and the crisis, we have determined to remain at Ramla, and we shall be rewarded by George riding over to Jaffa, to gain all possible intelligence with regard to our missing letters and future movements.

Our social monk is the perfect representation of a lazy friar, whose only occupation is teaching Flora, a young hound, her exercise. He is from Saragossa, where, he says, the national proverb is, " *La notte per dormire, il giorno per riposare.*"

DECEMBER 12TH.—We passed a very good night, and the morning's light revealed all the cobwebs and dust, of which we were last night unconscious. I was rather disturbed by, what I thought, the noise of camels, but I found it proceeded from a dove-cot close to my window; and certainly Asiatic turtle-doves coo much more mournfully than those of Europe: it is a sort of wail and moan, like a discontented, peevish wife. I think the monks must have added this establishment to the monastery, to put them out of conceit with domestic life.

Our gloomy apartment led to a tiny garden, full of lemon-trees in full bearing; the air was quite perfumed by the cedrate, and Minney and the Doctor went through the German lesson without hat or cloak, out of doors, in the middle of December.

George rode off to Jaffa, and we found a very pretty walk through an avenue of *ficus indicus*, which brought us to a grassy hillock, where we took up our quarters, and sent for our work and books; a good many of the female inhabitants of Ramla had made the same choice, and appeared to have sufficient occupation in watching our movements. Some little Arabs were playing at soldiers, with sugar-canes for muskets; and some little girls were made quite happy by my presents of needlefuls of red worsted. We had hoped to have our broken chairs repaired, but all the workmen of Ramla had been sent off to assist at the restoration of the fortifications of St. Jean d'Acre.

We anxiously expected the result of George's visit to Jaffa, and he found that the *obliging* Mons. Cuisinier, who, unasked, had proffered his services to forward our letters, had sent a large packet by a common muleteer conducting some pilgrims to the Greek convent, without a more specific direction; so we are now more tantalized than ever, from knowing that the letters are arrived, but having no means of communicating with the Greek convent.

We cannot ascertain what will be our fate about the Al Arish quarantine, but we shall set off to-morrow for Esdoud (the ancient Ashdod.) I felt struck at this convent, with the reflection, how the monks have the power of supporting privations, or rather the monotony of a monastic life, without a spark of religious enthusiasm, or at least without any deep respect and reverence for its truth. Indeed there is no sign of either among such of the monks as we have seen; they only appear like secluded and retired *Bourgeois*, without any intellectual or actual pursuit.

December 13th.—We left Ramla about twelve, after the monks had afforded us every possible hospitality; the now convalescent superior sent for George, to express his gratitude for the attentions of his doctor; to the latter he gave a pretty Bethlehem snuff-box.

The weather was charming on our first setting off; the *Viaggiatore Piccola*, as the monks named Minney, was a little shy of the umbrellas, which we were soon obliged to *déployer*, as the rain descended in torrents; and although our *impenetrable* cloaks proved worthy of their names, we saw our beds getting a sad soaking. The afternoon again proved fine, and a variety of game appeared so inviting, that our *padrone* thought himself justified in disregarding our nerves for the sake of *savoury meat* for our evening's re-past. We found Esdoud two miles further distance than had been reported, and we hoped so much might be gained on our journey of the next day.

The night had just closed in before we reached Esdoud; we could hardly see our way, when, on approaching the village, we were all startled, by a person coming up on horseback at full gallop. The darkness added to the surprise we all felt, when we perceived that it was an Arab soldier, who flew by, calling out loudly, and apparently regardless whom he rode over; he proved to be one of Mehemet Ali's messengers, conveying despatches to his son.

He passed us like lightning; we could only discern his large white teeth under the capuchin of his *bernouss*, which covered him in a most picturesque manner. The sudden manner in which he just appeared and then vanished, caused, I believe, an impression on all our minds, which I can no otherwise describe, but as of a phantom that whirled by us, or, as what one may conceive, to illustrate the idea of Death on the Pale Horse.

We were received by Denino with an unfavourable account of our quarters, which impression was indeed fully justified; the little room was so full of smoke, sheep and lamb skins, that we were some time before we could effect an entrance: anything so close as the atmosphere I never felt, from the combined smells of wool, oil, and tobacco. My first step was into a puddle.

When the smoke was a little dispersed, by the pan of ashes being removed, we discovered that the upper end of the room was raised, so that our beds could be placed out of the mud, but how, and where our baggage was to be disposed of, was a fresh puzzle; at last, another room was offered, in the village, for the gentlemen, smaller, and even less ventilated, but the ground was too damp to allow the alternative of encamping; so we determined to look on the amusing side of the question—viz., the dismay of Christine, and the surprise of the Arabian women, who had evidently never before seen a Christian woman.

No sooner was our supper concluded, and Minney and I had been left alone, than the whole female population of the neighbourhood poured in upon us, and they were more difficult to eject than either the sheep or the poultry. The shiek's wife had a very agreeable countenance, and inquired, by signs, the number of my children, which question I returned, and admired her pretty little girl, who then disappeared, as I hoped, for the night, and I trusted that the mother would quickly follow.

I was disappointed in both expectations ; the little daughter returned, with a baby in her arms, whom I was obliged to admire, and I felt they intended to pass the night in my room, or rather in hers, as she was the proprietor of this wretched cabin ; at last we were obliged to summon Denino, and make him interpret our wish of going to bed, with a civil hope of seeing them the next day.

Although at the risk of suffocation, we then fastened our door, which there was a constant attempt to open for a long time. At last Christine, being fairly awakened, got up to remonstrate ; but the interloper turned out to be a remarkably fat sheep, that had evidently been accustomed to the shelter of our apartment. Our musquito nets, I fancy, saved us from being perfectly devoured.

DECEMBER 14TH.—After a very much better night than we could have hoped for, we rose with unusual alacrity to get out of our den. George arrived with an indifferent account of his night's rest, and we heard a sad narrative on the part of the poor doctor, who, in addition to the winged enemies, had (in fancy, as we thought) seen a rat running over his coverlid, and the conviction (as he said) of the presence of many others " *qui soupiroient à mes oreilles.*"

He was soon assailed by all the sick and fanciful of the village for consultation ; his principal patient was a handsome Arab, who had nearly lost the sight of one eye, and who had hitherto been satisfied that a talisman, in the shape of a fine-sized pearl, hanging from his turban above the eye in question, would effect his cure. The doctor recommended as a substitute the constant use of cold water, with some little accessory, as there is no doubt that the want of cleanliness is the great aggravation of this species of ophthalmia.

After superintending for three hours the loading of our mules, the arrangements of which would by a European have been accomplished in as many quarters, we were fairly off, and passed in less than two hours a much better village than Esdoud, which last, remarkable in ancient history for resisting for months the invasion of Alexander, retains now no distinction but that of harbouring scorpions of a most venomous species.

We fortunately were in advance of the black and threatening clouds of rain which we saw bursting over the mountains of Judea; and our day's journey lay through a pretty country, richly cultivated. A good deal of ploughing was going forward, and in

one instance a camel was engaged, that
looked quite out of character, in agricultural
pursuit : the labour of turning the camel
every two minutes must have been much
greater than the mere manual labour of
turning up the ground where the rich yet
light soil offers such facility.

Dummy was more active than ever in
running up trees to gather switches to
punish our lazy mules, and then crouching
to make his back a firm support for mount-
ing on our awkward Turkish saddles ; he
was the perfect illustration of the dumb
slave in the Arabian Nights, and his quick-
ness of perception perfectly astonishing.
In coming into our room in the morning,
he had caught sight of himself in the little
looking-glass belonging to my dressing-case,
and looked perfectly bewildered ; but at last
ascertaining the cause of reflection, shrugged
up his shoulders with a mixed expression of
pity and dismay at his appearance.

During the day's journey he acted as pointer to our *chasseur*, who found plenty of sport in a country abounding in partridges, plovers, and rock and wood pigeons. We passed through forests of olives, not thickly planted, but affording very desirable shade and contrast to the country we had lately passed.

We reached the walls of Gaza about sunset; I never saw such a sky. On the left were masses of fleecy clouds, not of the dense character of our northern climates, but reminding us of the white smoke emitted by Mount Vesuvius at the eruption we had seen some months before. Behind a grove of beautiful palm-trees the sky appeared like a bright fire; one felt that it might have scorched the upper branches.

What a contrast between this burning climate and the country we had just left! No vegetation beyond that of palms and the *ficus indicus*, and everything denoting a tropical country.

George had remained at a little distance from the approach of Gaza, intent on adding to our pigeon pie, and on our arriving at the gates we found no *Cavasse*, or any one to shew us where Denino had made our quarters, and our Arabs conducted us to the khan, a regular warehouse built round a court, where we recognised our baggage, but no Denino, no Demetrius, no anybody that could tell us where to go. We all became very hungry and impatient, even to our poor horses, that tried to shake us off our saddles, for they were too tired to kick us off.

At last a figure advanced towards us, half Oriental, half European, offering his services, with a volubility truly Neapolitan, who informed us that he was the *Deputatore della Sanità* of Gaza, and that he was directed by the governor to express his regrets at his inability of lodging us *d'una maniera convenevole al rango*, but that already a warehouse was emptied for our reception, and that our kitchen was most conveniently situated in the open court, where a tent was also pitched.

This description did not quite realize our sanguine expectations of better lodging at Gaza; but the sheltered though unglazed windows, and a whitewashed wall, made our quarters appear luxurious after Esdoud.

The room was large enough to allow our fixing a rope across it, which enabled us to hang shawls and cloaks upon it, to afford George and ourselves independent *ménages* and *boudoirs*. Our *medico* and *artiste* were condemned to encamp in the court, and we were soon comfortably settled round a dining-table furnished by our obliging inspector of quarantine, whom we detained to supper, and a most amusing *convive* he proved, giving us an account of his past life and adventures, with all his Neapolitan vivacity.

His father had been a trader between Naples and Alicant, and his son, our guest, had succeeded to his father's profession, and for years with success.   A storm, however, wrecked both his ships and his fortunes, and at forty he had to begin the world again. He next found himself at Algiers, where he had some commercial relations; and at the moment when the French took possession of it, owing to his having some slight knowledge of Arabic, he became dragoman and a sort of *fournisseur* to Maréchal Bourmont, and in his employment made four thousand dollars.   He then was accused by some of the native residents of diminishing their commercial interests, thrown into prison, and condemned to twelve years' *galères*, but was released by Maréchal Bourmont's interference, who had then left the country, but the four thousand dollars were gone, " *non c'è.*"

He got transported with his family to Naples; again on the *pavé*, with nothing but *la divina clima* to console him, as the relations he found alive were as poor as himself. At last an old acquaintance at the *Douane* obtained a situation for him at Aleppo, whence he was again transferred to Beyrout, then to Damascus, where his pitiable condition, that of having a wife and three children to support on five piastres (1*s.* 3*d.*) a day, gained for him the sympathy of an *employé* of Ibrahim Pacha, and obtained for him the post of inspector of health in this miserable and unwholesome spot, with an ill-paid salary of three hundred piastres a month. All this he told us without any apparent complaint or attempt to work upon our compassion.

The thing he seemed most to lament was the impossibility of having his baby christened, out of reach as he was of any Catholic ecclesiastic, and having no feeling of community with the Greek church. "*Poveretta Marietta, che ha il nome ma non é Cristiana.*"

He had an equally anxious feeling to contend with, in the baneful effect of the climate on the eyes of his children, whom our doctor found in all the different stages of ophthalmia; his boy, whom he is endeavouring to get educated for a dragoman at an Arabic school, was the greatest sufferer; and upon the doctor betraying his apprehension for the sight of one of the poor boy's eyes, the poor father's feelings quite overcame him.

Had we given him a fortune he could not have appeared more grateful than for the ointment my little *pharmacie* enabled the doctor to compose. He assured us of the everlasting gratitude of *la mia Moglia, la mia Sposa, la mia Metà, la mia femmina,* and at last *la mia Vecchia,* by which variety of appellations he designated Signora Spada.

CHAPTER IV.

A visit from the Governor of Gaza, and his *suite*—
Our return visit—the Governor's stud—His harem
—The gates of Gaza—Singular conveyance—Our
camel—Travelling disasters—Uncomfortable lodgings, and unpleasant intelligence—*At home* in
the desert.

DECEMBER 15TH—With the hope of re-
ceiving our letters, and the advantage of
making Sunday a day of rest, we decided
on remaining at Gaza. George went to the
governor's to arrange our future caravan;
and we despatched a messenger with a
polite letter of inquiry to the French rene-
gade governor of El Arish, to ascertain

how far he was disposed to take a bribe, and allow us to escape the quarantine.

Minney and I then made ourselves very comfortable, and converted our barrack *en salon*, when we received a messenger to announce the governor's visit to "*our harem*." He soon followed, with two secretaries, three Negro slaves, and five Arab attendants, and squatted on my bed, *à la Turque*, surrounded by his staff, and inclined to look as dignified and condescending as his very ignoble countenance would allow.

Pipes and coffee were produced in as Oriental a fashion as our circumstances would permit; and then followed a curious and close inspection of every article our baggage contained. A phosphorus-box in my writing-case caused great surprise, not unmixed with alarm; the children's picture excited great admiration; but our governor persisted in his inquiries, why George had not my picture, as I was his only wife; and the information that Minney and I could read and write, filled him with great astonishment. His son (rather a good-looking youth of eighteen,) then joined us, and would sit on one of our camp-stools *à l'Européenne*, evidently with great discomfort to himself. He appeared in much awe of his governor (in our English acceptation); at last the room became oppressively close, from the smoke, and from its crowded state. When our visitors took leave, they exacted from us a promise that we, in return, would pay a visit to their harem in half an hour. We, however, began with the more interesting visit to the stables, where we saw two perfectly beautiful horses; one a young chestnut, which the governor offered to part with for fifty purses, about 225*l.* I longed to see George guilty of the extravagance of this purchase; though I suspect, by his having been tied by the four legs, he was not of a happy temper. The horse next him was a grey one, more advanced in years, but of still greater beauty. His head was the very *beau idéal* of perfection, and his long and bushy tail, like burnished silver; the stable itself was of the temperature of a European one, and did not differ in its arrangement, but in the absence of the wooden divisions for the stalls.

There were in all about twenty riding-horses; a good stud for the governor of this wretched place. He bears a tolerable character for one but lately promoted from the galleys of Damascus, by the favour (or caprice) of Ibrahim Pacha. He was very obliging in furthering the comforts of our journey, and reducing its expenses, *en revanche*. Spada informed us, he had observed " *son matti questi Franchi* to have left their riches and safe country to come and see our wretched existence, only to take

Ritratti." This impression was not made by Mons. Chacaton's drawings, but from the last European travellers having been Horace Vernet and his son, whom we unluckily missed on our first day's journey from Jerusalem, and in consequence probably lost much useful and agreeable information.

Giovannina, Spada's daughter, a nice-looking girl, of Minney's age, accompanied us as interpretess to Hadmin Hassan's harem. We were shewn into a pretty apartment, where we found two of his wives, rather *passées*, but with agreeable and expressive countenances, and more civilized manners than our Turkish friends at Nourri Effendi's; the elder one was mother to the young man whom we had seen before, and who pointed out three of his sisters, and then a very ugly, sallow-looking little woman as his wife, and begged me to look at her in the light, of which I did not at first make out the object. At last it was explained to me that, as a Frank, I must have some knowledge of medicine; and he wished me to prescribe, and account for her deep yellow hue, of which I communicated my suspicions, but recommended our *Medico*. This he pronounced impossible, as no man could enter the precincts of the harem; but the little jaundiced wife seemed determined to overrule her husband's objections, and have advice at the fountain head; and it was decided "*con licenza del superiore*," our doctor was to present himself at eight the next morning.

Young Abdul Hadmin offered us sherbet and coffee; and after our declining the pipe of friendship, he conducted us to his side of the harem, followed by the whole female part of the family, mounted (as it had just rained) on what may be described as very high pattens, or low stilts, and making them suddenly appear like a race of giantesses.

Minney attempted to shuffle on in a pair, much to the amusement of our entertainers.

In the first harem we were given chairs, but in this we squatted on the Persian rugs, and were asked to take off our bonnets, shew our hair, and display our ornaments : of the latter all that could be produced was Christine's gold watch and chain. They had intelligence enough to inquire whether Christine was not of a different country from ours ; but we quite failed in making them understand she was a Swiss, Inglese and Francese being their only European distinctions.

I forgot to mention how much I had fallen in importance since my first arrival at Gaza ; I had entered the town without George and my suite of nineteen mules and attendants, and as they saw by the firman we were English, I was reported to the authorities as a travelling wife of the English sultan. One would have imagined

the fact of a great people (as they acknow-
ledge us to be) being governed by a
woman, and that woman a young queen,
would not have been unknown even in
these parts.

DECEMBER 16TH.—Roused very early to
little purpose, as the camels for which we
engaged to pay an extra price if they
arrived before seven, never made their appearance till after *mezzo giorno.* We tried
to discover some interest in the locality of
Gaza, and were shewn the gates of the
mosque (which had been originally a
Christian church) as those which had been
carried off by Samson! I should think
they had been constructed within the last
century,* if any thing at Gaza bears so

---

* During the French occupation of Gaza, a General
Samson was a very active character; and in alluding
to the fact of the ancient gates, we found their original
celebrity confounded with the removal of the modern
gates by this French commander.

modern a date ; for although it boasts of having for so long withstood a siege by Alexander the Great, and of having been the capital of Palestine, except a few broken columns, not a vestige remains to attest its former consequence, and there is a total absence of the natural grandeur of feature that distinguishes Jerusalem and its immediate neighbourhood.

Mons. Chacaton contrived to make a very pretty drawing of a grove of palm-trees, and thus for himself lessened the misery of *attente* and idleness, under which we were all suffering. At last some of our camels were loaded, and our tartahuan elevated, a structure impossible to describe ; but as being like two punch show-boxes cut short, tied upon each side the camel, with the fronts facing each other, the closed parts being outside, and the back of the camel affording the separation and the means of entrance ; no wadding or lining, but the sharpness of the edge of the boards is taken off by spreading mattresses upon them.

Our first start was one of vast difficulty, for four men could not succeed in keeping our camel down ; even in this attitude we required a short ladder to scramble up, and a rope passed through the wooden laths to hold on. At last the signal was given to prepare us for *Gemala's* rising, which was not as great a shock as we had been prepared for, it was so gradual. The first motion was the elevation from his hind legs ; the second, from his knees in front ; and the third, entirely raised on his legs. I pitied the Turkish ladies who travel in this way to Mecca ; for at first starting, the motion is quite intolerable, like being at sea, the giddiness proceeding from the height at which one is raised, together with the swinging and creaking noise accompanying the machinery of a steam-engine.

Our camel, I fancy, had never borne such

a load as Minney, our mattresses, and myself,
and nearly forfeited his race's character for
forbearance. His first misdemeanour was
rushing into a hedge of cactus, which the
guide rather encouraged, I suppose, to save
his provision of corn. We expected every
moment to be knocked off, from the force
with which we went against it. In consequence, we were obliged to go through
the ceremony of making the animal kneel
down again, to have the cords freshly secured, and constantly to change our position
to keep the machine in proper balance.

I thought nothing could add to our
désagrémens, till an unexpected and soaking
rain came on. We felt our mattresses wet
through; and we saw the same disaster
extend to the rest of the baggage. In two
hours we hailed with delight a little bright-
ness in the sky at sun-set, and endeavoured
to persuade ourselves we were not wet
through; but a still heavier shower dis-

pelled all illusions ; and we heard that the
second tartahuan, containing Christine and
the doctor, was missing ; that another camel
had fallen down with our crockery, and
that we were two hours from the fountain,
designated as the spot at which we were to
encamp.

George got on beautifully with his dromedary, and quieted my fears of his catching
cold, and suffering from a return of ague,
by assuring me his *impenetrable* deserved its
name. For three successive hours, Minney
and I took to patience and silence.

At last, a light was to be distinguished ;
and great was our delight at finding we
were spared encamping on the damp
ground, and that we had reached the village
of Khan Yunez, where our new soldier-escort
found us quarters. And after passing
through a straggling village and dilapidated
court, we ascended a broad but broken
flight of steps ; and having threaded some

rather finely vaulted passages, we found ourselves in a very large building, lighted by a solitary lamp.

As soon as it enabled us to distinguish surrounding objects, we perceived that we had entered a somewhat ruined mosque, and that the lamp was hanging from rather a fine marble pulpit, with a flight of steps leading up to it. The certainty of partial shelter quite restored us. A sheik with a benevolent countenance attended us, and we made signs for fire, and in a short time we were sitting round one made on the stone pavement ; but as there was no chimney, and the materials were brushwood, we were almost stifled in our endeavours to dry ourselves, and had to contend with some lazy Arabs of the village, who took this opportunity of warming themselves, and kept half our party at a distance from the fire. The missing pair at length arrived, more frightened than hurt.

The alarm had thrown poor Christine into such a nervous state, that she arrived, crying, ill, and *trempée aux os*, the doctor, in vain, endeavouring to comfort her, and assuring her that the crockery alone had sustained fracture. In short, for the first time during our journey, she was perfectly helpless. At last, we found carpets and shawls in our baggage which had escaped the rain, and made out six couches, (for beds they could not be called,) but it was two in the morning before we could profit by them. In spite of all our difficulties, Denino contrived to feed us very satisfactorily, which was a great revival to our good humour and spirits.

Notwithstanding so much fatigue, my slumbers were not deep, as the rats had evidently been our immediate predecessors, and gave incessant proofs of their desire of regaining possession of their quarters. My inconvenient alarm at anything in the rat and mouse form, made me most selfishly keep up a constant jingle, by means of a tin basin, on the pavement, to alarm my enemies, and my poor family suffered in proportion. The muezlin calling the hours from the turret of our mosque, would have itself prevented our repose being very continued. I quite dreaded day, lest I should face my rats, but they had all discreetly retired with the moonlight.

DECEMBER 18TH.—Our messenger from Al Arish arrived, with the unsatisfactory answer from the Governor, that we must, if passing through his territory, be detained in quarantine for twenty-one days. There never was such absurdity as this, for no quarantine is in force at the sea ports nor in any other direction, and it is persevered in here from some crooked policy of Mehemet Ali's, from which unfortunate travellers suffer. It is intended, I suppose, to discourage the European intercourse with

Syria. We are, however, assured that, by a circuit of twenty miles, we may escape the cordon. Here, however, we must remain all day, to dry our mattresses, and increase our provisions. It was fortunate we came to this decision, for I should have probably knocked-up on the road, as, owing to the shaking and fatigue of the tartahuan, I found, on getting up, I was too ill and giddy to stand, and was delighted to follow our hakim's advice, of remaining all day in perfect repose and idleness.

I believe my absence from dinner was of general advantage, as our eggs had failed, and the fare was unusually scanty. What delights are real beds and sheets! It was almost worth making this expedition, to appreciate such restoration to *comfort*. What an odd word to adopt in a ruined mosque, full of dirt and rats! but so it is.

DECEMBER 19TH.—Found myself quite well enough to start; George's purchase of a pony for Minney, and our Arab soldier, *for a consideration*, allowing me to mount his beautiful pet horse, Kalid, has very much simplified matters. A bright and cloudless sky has encouraged us to hope we shall have no further repetition of our late disasters.

A messenger is just arrived from Jerusalem—no letters, alas! and every reason to believe that, owing to their having been put under cover to our Consul, they acquired an official appearance, and have been either intercepted by Greek emissaries, or destroyed by the government, who are always made suspicious by the arrival of European correspondence.

We set off, very heavy at heart, all prospect of hearing from our children being at an end, till we reached Cairo; on the other hand, we find that we have done well to come this road, as our purposed one, through Samaria and Galilee, was still dangerous, from insurrection, and that at Hebron four soldiers and the sheik were killed at the very time we should have been passing through; and that the Governor of Jerusalem had been obliged to shift his quarters till he could summon a fresh reinforcement of troops to subdue it. It is too provoking that the English steam-boat should be taken off the Syrian station, so that no communication for English agents, or means of passage for travellers is afforded, while Greek agents abound, in pay of Russia, and feeling the pulse of Syria, so as to profit by an advantage at the moment of the crisis of its fate, which all parties seem to agree will be at the period of the death of Mehemet Ali, an old man, upwards of seventy!

We were made fully aware of being among the Philistines, and were obliged to keep most diligent watch over our baggage, as *amateur* porters were in abundance, and we saw their taper fingers (by which these Arabs are much distinguished,) inserted into every accessible point of our baskets and boulahs. We escaped with only the loss of some cord, which we lived to learn was a very inconvenient one. They, in return, hinted we had appropriated some of their mosque matting, which, by-the-bye, they had removed on our first arrival, lest it should have been contaminated by our infidel touch.

At last we got off, and in an hour reached the confines of the real Desert. The first living inhabitants were very numerous, in the shape of rats, which appeared to have burrowed for miles in every direction; and to screen myself from such very disagreeable objects, I held my parasol close over my face, and trusted to Kalid's firm stepping. In this he did not deceive me, but caused me the not agreeable surprise of kneeling down very deliberately, and then rolling on the sand *les quatre pattes en l'air*.

This evolution had been sufficiently gradual, to afford me time to throw myself off, and out of the reach of such horse-play, only my poor saddle was the worse, and I resigned the reins of government into our squinting Solyman's hand. Our next incident was meeting with a very bright-coloured, but, I conclude, venomous serpent, from the attitude of vehement attack assumed by two of our followers, who with their strong clubs and vigorous blows soon destroyed it. They would have afforded a pretty study for an artist, with their eager countenances, and the graceful folds their loose drapery always assumes during any exertion; for, in painting, the outlines and colouring tell, while the absence of cleanliness, which, in Arab life, one is so constantly reminded of, is not felt.

During the first portion of our journey, we were constantly in fear of the patrouille of the cordon. That I might repose, or at least make the attempt, I again took to the

tartahuan, and with a little more success.
I left Kalid to Christine's lighter weight.

Two hours sooner than we anticipated,
(the sixth of our journey,) we saw a light,
and our three white tents most comfortably
pitched with a blazing fire in their front.
We rejoiced, under so fair a sky, at being
free from the shelter of Arab hospitality.
Our beds and furniture were soon disposed
of, and nothing could be more successful
than our first *at home* in the Desert.

Although a good deal of dew fell, it did
not penetrate the canvas of our tents, and
we fancied we had not slept so well for
weeks. The largest tent we made our
harem: in the next best were George, the
doctor, and the artist, and the third was
left for our servants, and only occupied by
Denino and Demetrius. The Arab servants
herded with the camel-drivers, and made
their abstemious meal apart. It seemed to
consist entirely of bread, like crumpets,

which they kneaded and baked on the stones. They appeared both to eat and sleep by snatches, and not a moment's general silence occurred among the party during the night, although there was no symptom of mirth, and Denino told us they were telling stories. So much for the beginning of our Arabian nights!

Just as we were going to close our tent for the night, Denino dragged in some skins and jars of water, of which most necessary article we found our attendants had made so small a provision, that our only security was in guarding our own. He suggested to us, that we must avoid, for the next forty-eight hours, being too extravagant as regarded ablutions, as it would be two days before we could reach a fountain : he did not, however, recommend the Mahometan substitute of sand on such occasions.

CHAPTER V.

Appearance of the desert—Fresh vegetables—An Arabic lesson — Our bivouac — Jewish feast of Tents—Camel's milk—Heat of the sun—A skirmish which is threatened with disagreeable consequences—Desert fare—Aerolites—Symptoms of discord.

DECEMBER 19TH.—Got off tents and all by ten o'clock, and, considering the impossibility of loading the camels, and taking up the tents, under two hours, we were rather satisfied at our activities; looked at *the real Desert* with great complacency, and found it not quite the still ocean of sand we had expected, as it was a good deal varied by

hillocks of sand, with bushes of heath, some
still in blossom, of a beautiful deep lilac,
with the softness of effect of chenille.   Frequently the sand, as it is drifted by the wind,
forms such beautiful patterns, having quite
the effect of a stamped design.

Although the weather was as warm as
the hottest day of an English July, yet it
was not oppressive ; the air was so light,
and a soft breeze blowing the whole day,
which enabled us to avoid making a midday halt.   Unluckily for our active intentions, the Arabs resisted continuing our
journey after four o'clock ; but after sundry
threats, and promises of *backshish* to Hadji
Barak, we proceeded eight miles further.

Our second night's encampment was
much sooner effected, as the beds and baggage began to know and find their own
places.   Our eating-table consisted of two
planks, supported at each end by a small
trunk, and was converted at night into

Minney's bedstead. Our *dinner-supper* was quite excellent; and Denino had so ingeniously contrived to plant cress and mustard in pots, and transport them invisibly, that we were probably the first travellers in the desert who had enjoyed the luxury of fresh vegetables.

Just before we arrived at our encampment, Denino had met a caravan from Suez, which had only been four days on its road. This made us wish to make it our route; but our Arab chief and our soldier murmured quarantine, the possible confiscation of their camels, and no redress ! It was tantalizing to think that our road should so nearly skirt Mount Sinai and the Red Sea, without being able to distinguish them, and knowing that the distance from Cairo was the same. After a great deal of discussion with our chief, and promises of additional pay, we made some impression.

Our Arab soldier, whose *début* had been

most respectful, in consequence of George having given him his pipe to smoke, (which had quite compromised our dignity and authority), had become so insolent, that he announced his decided opposition; however, upon assuring and convincing him we could dispense with both his and Kalid's services and society, he changed his tone; and being perfectly disinclined to a solitary journey to Cairo, he said he should be wanting in duty to us and his pacha, were we to proceed without his escort.

We had the luxury of finding that our *moya* (water) might now be used *ad libitum*, as the next day would bring us to a fountain. Denino gave Minney a long Arabic lesson; my jaws are much too stiff to bear the extraordinary exertion of the pronunciation; the language is so emphatic, sonorous, and guttural, that it requires the united efforts of lungs, throat, and lips, to ask the name of a place. I found the word *taib*, (c'est bien,) of the most general service, only varying the tone as I conceived the occasion required. During Minney's lesson I was much amused at our half-blind Solyman, in a low key, repeating each word after Denino, and correcting his pronunciation; the criticism was fortunately lost on the teacher.

Nothing could be more military and picturesque than our bivouac, encamped in a narrow and sheltered valley. Our soldier is a Bedouin, and a great dandy in his toilet; his *bernouss* and dress entirely white, fine in texture, and relieved with a narrow red border : he quite bears out the character of an Arab, with whom care for his horse is always the master feeling; as Kalid is cleaned, coaxed, and fed, before he thinks of himself, and in the short allowance of water, Kalid takes the first share, and from the same vessel as his master.

An additional motive for wishing to reach

Suez is, that we run the chance of profiting by the Indian steam-boat, which leaves Suez on the first of the month, and may land us at Cosseir, which is within three days of Thebes, and thus afford us more time and greater variety of country.   One feels every circumstance attending the temporary though complete shelter of a tent so calculated to induce a comparison with that of our earthly pilgrimage ; surrounded by one's children, servants, cattle, provisions, and household goods,—one's home of a few hours seems so calculated for one of permanent abode ; the sounds of early preparation for departure are sometimes heard before the eyes are as yet closed in sleep, and every thing combines to remind one that we are arrived but to depart !—a few hours later all trace on the sandy space afforded by our late habitation consists of the few stones which had served for our fires, or to confine with more security the

cordage of our tents. Never had we experienced the forcible illustration of the
transitory state of our existence, which our
present mode of journeying affords.

The Jewish feast of Tents or Tabernacles
is believed to have been appointed for the
purpose of commemorating the long pilgrimage of trial and difficulty which the
Israelites, for their disobedience, were compelled to undergo in the Desert before at-
taining possession of the Promised Land;
may not an incentive to future exertion
and ultimate reward be connected with the
commemoration of deliverance from peril,
and the final attainment of the one great
object of their journeyings?

DECEMBER 20TH.—We found our encampment had been made close to what appeared
to have been the beds of some large and important rivers; and our guide pointed at one
as the direction of Al Arish. We contrived
to be off in even better time; and a drove of

wild camels coming up to us at breakfast-time, Denino suggested to us *du lait de chamelle*, which was really very good, and less strong than the goats' milk we had tasted at Chamouny only a few months before.

In spite of the early hour at which our journey began, we were made most sensible of the already warmer climate, and by twelve the sun almost scorched us. We endeavoured to be patient, and were supported by the conviction that we should soon arrive at the fountain, the *point de reunion*, with Denino and the early detachment of our camels; but from a want of understanding with our guides that there were two fountains at equal distances but far asunder, our Hadji brought us to the fountain on the left, and after suffering all the dread of having missed our road, and being separated from all our party who could interpret for us, we rode on for three hours more, under what even *acclimaté*

George allowed to be the furnace of a tropical sun.

One never before understood the eagerness one has heard described, of endeavouring to track footsteps in the sand, or trace a watercourse. We were constantly misled by the track of some wild camels we afterwards found browsing on the stunted heath, for there was no longer any of the beautiful species we had admired the day before. We then reached what had evidently been the bed of a river, and our Arabs called out quarantine, pointing to its course in that direction.

A la fin des fins, we saw the tartahuan in advance stand still, which indicated that they had arrived at some incident, and a very disagreeable one it proved. It was a skirmish between Denino and his accompanying party of Arabs. They had provoked him by hastily unloading the baggage to water the camels, and his own irritable temper, aggravated by the long exposure to the sun, had made him deal blows to the right and left.

Against one man he had used the butt-end of his gun, and in plucking out a piece of his beard had inflicted the greatest insult to a Mussulman, who with a companion had flown over the hills, (for at this point the sand banks quite deserve the name,) threatening to be revenged by denouncing us at the cordon in Turkey; in short, the confusion was quite overpowering.

The clearness of the atmosphere enabled us to keep sight of them in their flight for a considerable time, though at length we became quite unable to decide whether they were still bent on taking their threatened revenge for the insults they had received, or whether, as our hopes made us willing to believe, they had thought better of it, and were retracing their steps. The anxiety with which we watched them was intense during the few moments in which, though they were clearly in motion, not one of us could tell which way they were going; till at length the gradual lessening of their forms, and soon after, their total disappearance, confirmed our worst fears, that, instead of being able to continue our journey at pleasure, we were doomed to drag out a twenty-one days' imprisonment in the merciless walls of the Al Arish quarantine.

The description I heard of Denino's violence perfectly disqualified me from taking the repose in the shade I had so eagerly looked forward to. In short, we twenty-six souls were all in *emoi* with our varied emotions; and to make the climax to our disasters, there was no prospect at half-past three of our prosecuting our journey, from the length of time required to re-load our camels; so *bon gré, mal gré*, we were obliged to halt, after a positive advance of only four hours.

Hadji Barak returned, having succeeded in overtaking and persuading our two threatening and fugitive Arabs to return. After having talked at and mortified Denino, I became better satisfied. The worst used Arab shewed me his wounded arm; and after affording him every possible sign 'of commiseration, and dividing with him the piece of bread I happened to be eating, he kissed my hand, placed his on his breast and head, and looked half recovered. However, I made our doctor come forward to perfect the cure.

Whether the now crest-fallen Denino was jealous of the bandages and attentions, or had not *la tête à la cuisine*, but so it was: in chopping some meat he let the knife come down upon his hand with so much force, that through the nail he nearly severed the joint of the thumb; this was a more serious blow than the one he had inflicted on the Arab; and the doctor was obliged to be peremptory in his treatment, as the cut was on dangerous ground, leading to a lock-jaw.

We had at least the advantage of being near a spring capable of alleviating the feverish symptoms in our caravan; in short, all the ill-luck of this *Friday* quite justified the usual superstition respecting the day. At night all assumed a more tranquil, if not a more cheerful aspect; we only had the momentary alarm raised by Christine of hearing sounds, " *Des Arabes ennemis peut être.*"

Our desert fare quite belies all I ever heard described, for which we must do justice to our chef Denino. Two large, or rather long baskets of chickens, have travelled with us from Gaza, and I quite rejoice in their progressive destruction, not, as might be expected, from pure *gourmandise*, but from knowing, from tartahuan experience, how to sympathise for their incessant jerking and swinging on camel-back.

DECEMBER 21ST.—We all set out together, as Hadji Barak, our second in command, insisted that we were in a dangerous neighbourhood, of which we greatly doubted the fact, as we were in the vicinity of a fountain, which must cause it to be a place of general caravan resort ; but Denino was too much of an invalid to allow his being sent off early. The weather was much more temperate, and we persevered in making nine hours' journey to make up for our loss of time the day before. The desert became much more stony, and the doctor picked up some aerolites with which he was much delighted, and which he generously shared with us *un*-geologists.

About four we imagined we saw a fine range of mountains to the left, but this turned out merely the effect of *mirage*, to Minney and myself quite a new object. She required consolation at that moment, as she had much taken to heart the discovery she had made that her pony was not shod. She took to tears when we objected to her walking during the hottest part of the day, to save *Yunoz's* hoofs.

Our encampment and dinner proceeded as usual; for *dessert*, Demetrius informed us that his countryman, the snuff-merchant, who was one of our caravan, separated from us after twelve to-morrow, as the direct road to Cairo was five days, and round by Suez it would be eight. This shook our purpose; for we felt the *chance* of securing a passage to Cosseir and the peep at the Red Sea not worth the sacrifice. We summoned a council of war, and *our general* informed us that the distance from our present point, by both routes, was quite equal, and that we had been completely misinformed.

This of course kindled the smouldering wrath of Denino against our Greek, who communicated an equal portion to the merchant. He laid the fault to the soldier, who wished, for some purpose of his own, to avoid going through Suez, and in a short time we had loud sounds of discord in the camp. It was quite the case of " Greek meeting Greek," and the actual "tug of war" was so strong, that George was obliged to interfere, both for motives of peace and our night's repose, of which we had rather fallen short the night before.

CHAPTER VI.

Fog and cold—The necessity of discipline—Marks of
a wild animal—The Philistines and the Ishmaelites
—Our employments—Meeting a caravan—Inconvenience of watering the camels—Beautiful situation of our encampment—A solitary robber—
Wild partridges—We approach the Red Sea—Our
impressions and reflections—Christmas-day in the
Desert.

DECEMBER 22ND.—We sent two of our
tents forward by seven o'clock, and by the
meritorious effort of dressing by candlelight,
we followed an hour later, but with much
difficulty, as we had so thick a fog that the
sun was quite obscured, and we could only
distinguish the marks of our *early* camels'

feet a few yards before us. The cold was so great that we could not tie a string, our fingers were so benumbed. But with all this the relief from the heat of the day before was very enjoyable.

We made a lazy young Turk, who had begged at Gaza to join our caravan, lead my horse. He confesses himself a deserter from the Turkish army, and his extreme laziness is quite amusing. He shuffles on in his slippers, and as they occasionally become imbedded in the deep sand, he seems to hold a debate with himself as to whether he shall suffer the fine of stooping for recovery.

We found it necessary to yield to the necessity of *practical* discipline among our troop, and on this said youth our *Cavasse* first practised. The result was satisfactory, for on arriving at our night's station he began to pitch the tent without assistance, but with the door towards the wind. On being desired to stop, and assist in putting up another in the right direction, he went on very steadily, knocking in pegs he knew were to come out, that he might not have the trouble of changing his position. He said, laughingly, that he had suffered so severely from the cold in the morning, that had his blood not been warmed by the *Cavasse's* discipline, he probably should have been unable to proceed. All this was accompanied with so much drollery of countenance, that it formed quite a contrast to the gloomy melancholy of our Arab escort.

We observed footsteps of a large animal on the sand, supposed to be those of a hyena, and I was rather hurt at the doctor not allowing that the sounds we heard last night, after our fires were extinguished, proceeded from anything more savage than a wild cat.

We were sadly disappointed at finding, by the little progress our *cuisine* had made, that Denino had not preceded us more than half an hour, owing to the roguishness of our guides, who had conspired to arrive together. Such cowards are this class of Arabs, and with such an absence of good faith, that they cannot be trusted for a moment; they appear to combine slavishness with tyranny.

It is singular how completely the ancient characteristic of the Philistines and the Ishmaelites is preserved, and that the latter's " hand is yet raised against every one, and every one's hand against theirs." They are in a constant state of suspicion and apprehension of each other; and although they may purloin from and cheat Europeans at convenient opportunities, yet they repose the most unbounded confidence in their promises, and never appear to measure Christian good faith by the Mussulman standard. In travelling through the Desert on the Sabbath, (with much regret at so doing,) we speculated as to whether we might not, in our present approach to the direction of the Red Sea, be traversing part of the actual wilderness where the manna fell, and that in double portions on the Sabbath eve, to inculcate more strongly the suspension of all labour, and the consequent consecration of that day of rest and holiness.

The latter part of our journey brought us to a very picturesque outline of mountains, in form rather like those of Wicklow, and under them we made our bivouac; after supper, Minney read to us portions of Scripture, alluding to points connected with the wanderings of the chosen people.

It was very amusing to observe the different employments allotted to us by our chief, Denino, as suitable to our several capacities, and in about as many languages. To the doctor he called, "Herr Bendiner Wollen sie die Huhner waser geben;" to

our artiste, "Mons. Chacaton, voulez-vous
bien enfoncer les picquets ?" " I say, colonel,
will you watch the saucepan, while I go pick
up more sticks ?"   " Signorina, avete la piccola lampa, e la chiava della cantina ?"
La Signorina, when once in the tent, is
invited by Christine' to lay on the cloth, and
lay out the contents of the canteen ; all I
am asked to do is, to help to make the beds,
and serve out currant-jelly and *mishmish*.

Before we separated we sent for our Hadji,
to tell him we would not again submit to be
treated as we had been that day, when our
intention of sending off Denino by early
dawn, to forward our arrangements, had
been frustrated by their obstinacy ; that we
would complain of him at Cairo, give little
backshish, &c., if he continued to thwart
our plans and progress. He said a great
deal in return, and we looked as if we
understood some part of it ; and by placing
taib at every pause he made, we came to

an understanding of better things for the morrow.

DECEMBER 23RD.—Succeeded in getting half the party two hours in advance, and passed our first six hours without *break of country* or shadow of interest. At length we distinguished a large number of camels, which alarmed our guides, till George's telescope enabled him to pronounce them loaded. This seemed to dissipate all alarm.

The prospect of meeting a caravan of thirty camels was very enlivening, for at a considerable distance we were able to reckon that number. I began calculating what friends and acquaintance it might include. Minney jumped at once to the conclusion that it must be Lord Harrowby and Lord Sandon pleasuring *northwards*, in search of a more temperate climate towards the approach of the rainy season, for we had read at Athens, in the papers, that they were gone to Cairo. The result was cruelly prosaic; nothing but Arab merchants returning from Cairo, and their load only barley and water-skins. This, however, we could only surmise, as no sort of communication took place between the Arabs of either caravan, and the only exchange of words was between our Greek and one of their party, from whom he made the inquiry of the distance to Suez. The answer of three days corresponded more than we desired to the previous assurances of our guides.

About half an hour later we heard the report of a fire-arm, which of course produced alarm among our Arabs, of which I was by no means divested. Our Cavasse was desired in return to fire his pistol, the approved manner of shewing we were not frightened, and no further shot occurred.

We soon afterwards reached our place of rest, found our tents pitched, and our fire burning briskly: although our early baggage had preceded us two hours, they had only gained an hour in advance; however, we were grateful for that improvement, and rather anticipate a curtailed journey for to-morrow, as the camels are to make an early watering expedition, and this operation consumes so much time, that we shall have no chance of renewing our day's journey in tolerable time.

We made a good fight against watering the camels at all, as our skins and jars were by no means exhausted. But our Hadji took to tears (or affecting them), tearing his beard, assured us his camels would die, &c., and further contention was useless.

DECEMBER 24TH.—The spot where we encamped was really beautiful, hills sur-rounded us on all sides, and the morning sun had a fine effect in producing the most beautiful tints. We crossed in the early part of our journey the rocky and rather picturesque course of a river, though hardly

qualified to be called so, from its dryness,
said by Laborde to be the Arish. The
features of the country reminded us much
of those about Buxton, where the beauty
of Matlock ceases.

At a turn of the path we met a well-armed,
solitary Arab, whom Denino questioned as
to the part of the country he came from,
and his answer was so confused and contradictory, that there was little doubt of his
being one of the Desert robbers, looking out
for easier plunder than our caravan was
likely to prove, as our table of statistics
stood at twenty-four camels, one horse, one
pony, twenty-six *live* chickens, and twenty-
three human beings.

We saw some very wild partridges, upon
which George wasted some gunpowder; at
each failure our *farçeur*, the young Turk,
exclaimed " *Ma fishe !*" " nothing," in a most
insulting tone of exultation, while he seized
my horse's bridle very sharply, as Kalid was

rather alarmed by the firing, which caused him to swerve and rear so suddenly at the edge of a very rocky and awkward path, that I felt my nerves somewhat shaken.

The remainder of our day's journey was very tedious, for the difficulty of finding a favourable point for our encampment made Denino prolong his march to the summit of a deep sandy range, where we found fuel very scarce and the night very cold.

DECEMBER 25TH.—We had great fear of our Christmas-day proving a broiling one, as the night's dew on our tent was completely dried by the power of the sun at eight o'clock. When we proceeded on our journey our apprehensions, however, were soon dispelled by a strong north wind, which the Arabs considered as the forerunner of rain. We proceeded, however, all in high spirits. The monotony of the Desert seemed past. To our left we saw the lofty ranges of mountains on which rests Mount Sinai.

The features of the country were all changed, and the Arabs were continually pointing, and crying out, " Suez."

At last we came in sight of the Red Sea, at some twenty-five miles distant. We seemed again approaching civilization—the current of our ideas took a fresh turn, and we were all more or less excited. We rode on alone, and occasionally re-united to communicate our impressions.

Our road lay over a vast, elevated plain. Three Arabs were in advance of us, patrolling the country half a mile a head, and appearing at the same distance from each other; there was no track but that made by the camels of our camp-kitchen caravan, which, owing to the nature of the ground, it was difficult to discover, but we moved on absorbed in thought, our eyes fixed alternately on Mount Sinai and on the spot we supposed to be Suez. The weather still continued beautiful, but the day seemed endless, and the distance from Suez appeared to increase in proportion as we advanced.

The evening closed in with every appearance of storm and rain, and at that moment we could nowhere discover, even with the telescope, any sign of an encampment. At nightfall our Arab scouts had wandered so far before us, in search of Denino, that they were far out of hearing, and we several times mistook some lighter object for our white tent; but all was illusion, except a very dark cloud, which at length dissolved in rain immediately over our heads, and which seemed to extend to a little distance only.

We jumped off our horses, exercised our newly-acquired talent of making a sort of gurgling noise, to make our dromedaries kneel, took off their saddles in most military style, and seated ourselves under the only bush that could be found, (and which we, half an hour later, converted into fire-wood,)

and unfurling all the umbrellas and para-
sols we could collect, contrived to shelter
ourselves and our bedding, while, (under
veteran George's orders,) the only tent in
our division of the baggage was raised. In
a short time we were all under it, lamenting
such a sad benighted position on a Christmas night, and sympathising with the probable distress and wanderings of Denino,
occasioned by our non-appearance.

The tent could not be sufficiently extended to allow my bed to be put up, but
we contrived, by general and individual con-
cessions, to make up six stations of repose ;
and as our canteen contained tea, brandy,
and sweetmeats, besides hard biscuit, we determined not to go to bed quite supperless.

George consoled himself by thinking a
banyan day might for once prove wholesome;
Minney, by convincing herself that the
variety this would offer to any future or
past Christmas fare, was very desirable. I

was less easily satisfied, and determined on a search for portable soup, and boiling it in the tea-kettle. I found the doctor and the artist very willing to assist me; and preparing the way, by collecting sticks, for which they in vain summoned the lazy young Turk to assist, who, although the rain had by this time ceased, they discovered on the sheltered side of the tent, snoozing most comfortably, and half buried in sand. He was certainly the Turkish counterpart of the fat boy in Pickwick.

All at once sounds were heard; we became breathlessly attentive, and the voice of Hadji Barak was soon recognised. He came to our tent door, shaking the drops of rain from his picturesque tartaned drapery, and by his gestures, and a few Arab words the doctor had contrived to make himself master of, we made out he had distinguished the fire our Arabs and drivers had lighted for themselves, at some little distance from us, and that we were only at half an hour's walk from the other encampment.

This most welcome information was soon followed by Denino, in *propria persona*, repeating all this information, and inquiring what he was to do with this too distant Christmas feast, which he had left hot, and *très appétissant*, and suggesting that we should move our encampment to the kitchen division. This I resisted, on the principle of the mountain and Mahomet, which seemed singularly appropriate; and during the description of our intended repast, George's palsied energies revived, and he determined on marshalling all our Arabs, under Denino's orders, to the other camp, to transport the dinner to ours, when a *rechauffé* might take place at our now very good fire.

This was done in so efficient a manner, (for I fancy the distance was not half what the tired limbs of Hadji Barak made him imagine,) that by nine o'clock our dinner was transferred, dry and hot, to our quarters ; and great was our surprise, when it proved the sort of dinner we might have been satisfied with in civilized Europe, five roast chickens, (being computed to make one turkey,) *bread sauce*, beside bouillie soup and vegetables, and a very good sort of pudding, meant to represent a plum, but in which dried apricots were a very improved substitute for plums ; in short, there never was such a caterer as Denino.

We could not keep our early hours on the preceding day, but really passed a merry Christmas evening, enhanced by the contrast our prospects had presented so short a time before. The other tents were by this time pitched, and we made the gentlemen a *coffee-room* on this occasion, to give time for our harem-camp to be restored to its general mode of arrangement.

CHAPTER VII.

Journey to Suez—The British Hotel—Mahomedan
pilgrims—Egyptian plagues—An Arab marriage
—The Consular agent—English news—The town
of Suez—Hadjis—Tedious journey—Deep excavation—Hyenas.

DECEMBER 26TH.—In spite of somewhat
damp tents, and not very dry sand, we all
met at breakfast, in the best possible health
and spirits, which the pure air of the Desert
certainly inspires.

We felt great satisfaction in looking forward to a short day's journey to Suez,
which appeared five or six miles off, within

a short ride, but here, as on many other occasions, we were deceived by the clearness of the atmosphere. It took us five hours to reach Suez, the journey being somewhat prolonged by the extended tour we were compelled to make to avoid the quicksands and estuaries, which extend for many miles from Suez.

At half-past three we arrived, and found ourselves, as we entered the town, in an atmosphere of dirt, insects, and offensive smells, and from the effect produced by the half-ruined miserable appearance of the exterior of what is distinguished as " the British Hotel," we were agreeably surprised at finding very clean, comfortable-looking bed-rooms. The entrance of this oriental dwelling being hung with advertisements, of—" Guinness' Porter" and " India Pale Ale," seemed vastly incongruous, and put whatever poetical ideas we might have indulged in, most strangely to flight ; and we met with the disappointing reality of hearing that our steam-boat had started the day before for Cosseir, anticipating by a week its usual departure, on the first of the month.

We determined, however, to see all we could of the Red Sea, in tint *deep blue*, and till sunset we had a delightful stroll on its shores, picking up shells in great abundance and variety, but not succeeding in seeing the beautifully and brilliantly-coloured fish we had heard so much described. Though we saw the setting sun, we did not observe that it assumed the form of a column or pillar of light, by which some travellers have been struck, thus associating this appearance with that of the pillar of fire which served the Israelites to travel by night as in the day.

The place did not possess any sort of beauty; but it borrowed a temporary interest from the circumstance of its being the season at which Hadjis of every country had assembled to embark for their pilgrimage to Mecca, and the varied form and colour of their encampments (chiefly made on the sea-shore) produced the most picturesque effect it was possible to imagine. This pilgrimage included specimens of every variety of national and oriental costume. To these Hadjis we (perhaps uncharitably) attributed the *extraneous* population of every *un*-nameable insect; for Greece, Turkey, and Syria, were clean and sweet, in comparison with this our first introduction to Egyptian plagues and customs.

During our walk homewards, we were accosted by two good-humoured-looking men, who had picked up half a dozen words of Italian, and, inquiring if we were English, added, "*Buona perchè Inglesi sempre sempre bravi.*" This acknowledgment proved quite an agreeable little incident, as the people of these countries are in general little *prèvenant* or communicative, and we felt quite proud of this courteous appreciation of the English character.

In passing through the very dirty street which led to our inn, we heard a very pretty Tyrolese air, sung by some hidden performer, which national music had the effect of quite affecting the doctor, and after the dreadful discord of Arab music, even our *un*-German ears were very agreeably refreshed.

Our dinner was exactly what we might meet with at Canterbury, rather better than it would have been at Dover, and on a most liberal scale; but mulligatawny soup, round of beef, and heavy plum-pudding, were too substantial substitutes for our good and wholesome Desert fare. Before it was quite ended, the sound of drum and tabret attracted us to the door of the hotel, and we found that an Arab marriage was taking place, by the light of coloured lamps and torches,

the former hung on poles, and the cry of—
" the bridegroom is coming," was another
instance of the constant recurrence of familiar images used in Scripture ; and he was
thus announced, as going forward to meet
the bride at the mosque, where both proces-
sions were to join. The bridegroom was
conducted between the other Arabs, dressed
like himself, in scarlet *caftans* and white
turbans, but he looked the very image of
grief, and appeared more like a criminal
pinioned for execution, than a *nouveau marié.*

Fancy had full scope to imagine blighted
hopes and forced marriage, but the exces-
sive din of drumming and singing made one
very unpoetical.

We were very much disgusted with the
bullying conduct of our host, who wantonly
levelled one of the poles supporting the
lamps, which broke into a thousand pieces,
scalding the bearers with hot oil. It should
be observed, that the upright supporters

had shorter pieces of wood running hori-
zontally across them, like the military bells
often seen in a band of music, on which
latter were suspended about twenty lamps
altogether. The confusion which followed
in the immediate ranks of the procession
prevented the offender from being ascertained, and I think it was very fortunate, as
their number, which must have been several
hundreds, might have taken justice into
their own hands, against so very small a
proportion of Europeans.

I got home as quickly as I could, but our
gentlemen went on to the mosque. The
scene had been by far the most picturesque
and characteristic I could have conceived,
and it was continued for three hours.

We found that we could not set out at the
early hour we proposed, for as every drop of
fresh water comes from Cairo, and its sale is
only twice a day, at the hours of our nine
and three, ten o'clock is the earliest hour at

which we can start. The Consular agent, a very obliging Mr. Levecke, came to see us, and very kindly promised to expedite matters, by making over some of his provision of water to Hadji Barak.

Mr. L. brought a large file of English papers and magazines, destined for Indian readers. This was a most unexpected treat, although after thirty days had passed without a communication of any kind from Europe, the dread of one's eye glancing to bad news connected with those at home, preponderated over every other feeling. An account of the Duke of Wellington's severe illness was the first article that struck us in the newspaper of the latest date, and a subsequent report of his death written on the cover of the packet, was of most dispiriting effect ; but Mr. Levecke was able to tell us that he had heard that morning from Cairo a verbal contradiction as to the full extent of such a calamity. A further search into the older newspapers brought us to the important subject of the Queen's intended marriage with Prince Albert, her cousin ; the very same good-looking prince we had remarked at St. Peter's a few months before, as presenting, in expression of countenance, such a contrast to his companion, Don Miguel, notwithstanding the share of good looks possessed by the latter.

Although our host was in our bad books, George called on him to furnish supper and claret, that we might loyally drink our young Queen's health. The wine was so dreadfully sour, that our visitor, Mr. Levecke, was obliged to decline doing more than appear to go through the form of drinking our patriotic toast.

DECEMBER 29TH.—We had time to make another little stroll by the sea-side, where several vessels were preparing to embark their pilgrim passengers.

The town of Suez seems fast tumbling to

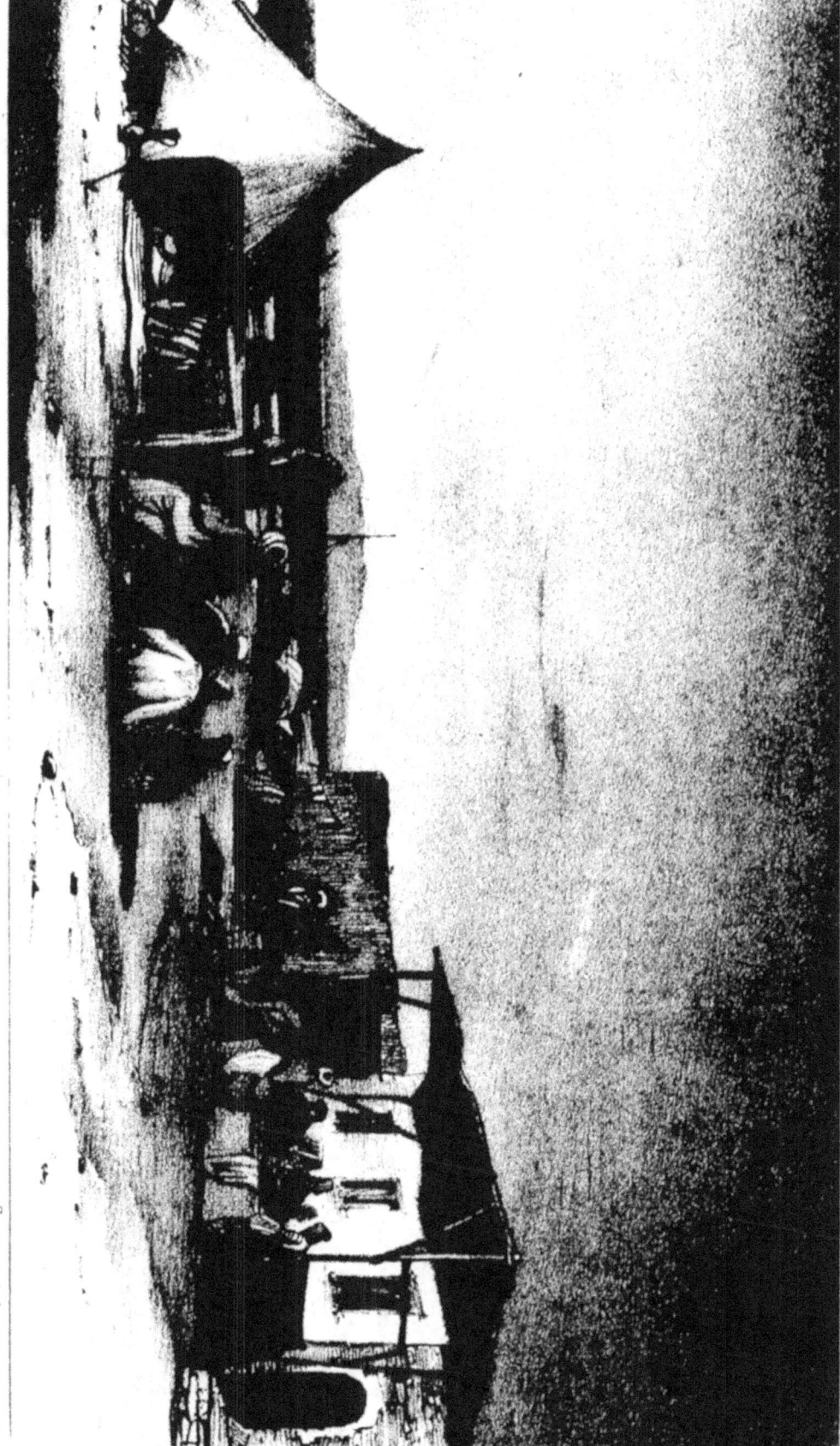

VIEW OF SUEZ

London Published by Henry Colburn, 13, G^t Marlborough S^t 1841

decay, and one felt so much for what poor Lord and Lady S——n must have gone through during their two months' forced residence at this wretched place, and that too in the very heat of the summer. We are told, however, that Europeans are much encouraged to improve the place, as the station of the steam-boat makes it so general and advantageous a position, and that almost everything may be found at Suez, from the increasing facility of communication with Cairo, from whence every necessary of life is brought, while Suez itself is completely unproductive.

Our caravan *got under weigh* at twelve. In spite of the temptations offered us, in the way of station-houses, vans, and donkey litters, provided for the travellers to and from India, we preferred keeping to our tents, notwithstanding a little patriotic remorse at not adding our mite of encouragement to Mr. Hill's Desert arrangements

The road from Suez was enlivened by our meeting numerous caravans of Hadjis, some included the harems in their suite; and several camels were actually piled with female slaves who, muffled in their yashmacks, were elevated on the baggage to a height perfectly alarming, while the wives travelled in tartahuans, which I suppose they manage better than we could contrive to do, as they really appeared to *repose* on their mattresses, an object we never could achieve. I suppose Turks are allowed to tighten their *domestic cords* to a degree Europeans could not indulge in; for the swerving of the machine appeared to be much lessened by their method of securing them.

After one hour's progress we made a halt at a fountain, but of such brackish water that the camels drank but little, though allowed to do so *à discretion.* It was a regular watering establishment, not like the wild spots in our former desert; and the scene of contention for the foremost places, by the caravans that met, was very stirring and amusing : some of the conductors fell into the water, from their eagerness to fill the skins.

The wish to get in advance of others seems as prevailing in the Desert as in the civilized world, but the Arabs have the advantage, as their opportunities of getting forward are more frequent than usually occurs in these our reformed times.

We only made a five hours' journey on an uninteresting, broad, beaten track ; in short this is the *Hounslow road* to Cairo, and quite of a different character to our late unfrequented Desert.

DECEMBER 28TH.—Set off early, determining upon a thoroughly long day's journey, to enable us to reach Cairo the next day. We found our nine hours' journey most unusually tedious, from the monotony caused by the straightness and uniformity of the road, which must have certainly been the sixth of a mile broad, and consisted of about twenty distinct camel paths, presenting no variety, or any object but camel bones. It was impossible to go one hundred yards without passing one of these huge skeletons, and yet not a dying or sick camel did we meet with. I suppose that it is in the hot season that the mortality must be so extensive. Fortunately the birds and beasts of prey are so numerous, that not an instance occurred of one's sight or smell being offended. The whole road was said to be burrowed by rats; but we saw none. I believe they emigrate from the interior of the Desert, and fix on this spot as their *pays de cocagne.*

We found Denino encamped near an excavation, which had been made by Mehemet Ali in hopes of obtaining water, which (unfortunately for us) turns out to be only the half-way spot from Cairo. This excavation is at least two hundred feet deep and one hundred wide. It was next to impossible to look down it, it was so trying to one's steadiness of head ! It was a sort of waking night-mare. We were obliged to take additional precautions in tethering the camels and horses, who, in their midnight peregrinations might fall into what appeared so bottomless a pit.

One regrets much that this very laborious and desirable undertaking should have failed, as no trace of water was discovered. It is believed that the Arabs of this district are acquainted with the positions of springs in this part of the Desert, but carefully conceal their knowledge from others. The number of wild beasts that frequent this part of the country almost prove the existence of springs. We were quite disturbed at night by the howling and contention of the hyenas for the bones that had remained strewn around our kitchen establishment. I was too idle to get up and look about me, but our gentlemen described them as very savage and wild-looking animals.

CHAPTER VIII.

Journey to Cairo continued—English inn in the Desert
  —Divine worship—Pilgrims in want of water—
  Donkey chairs—First view of Cairo—Impressions
  on entering the city—Singular petrifactions—Mr.
  Waghorn — Mehemet Ali's resources — Cairo
  donkey-boys and donkeys — Egyptian mules —
  Mosque of the Sultan Hassan — The citadel —
  Massacre of the Mamelukes—Court of Yousouff
  —New mosque—New palace of the viceroy—
  Punishments—Beautiful garden—Egyptian necro-
  mancy—A wedding.

DECEMBER 29TH.—Alas! still too far from
Cairo, for exertions like those of yesterday
to compensate for the fatigue we underwent ;
for although we determined upon a moderate
day's journey, and terminating our Desert

expedition at leisure, yet owing to the hard road and the illness and fatigue of two of our camels, we were nine hours reaching our encampment.

Poor Kalid seemed quite knocked up with his fourteenth consecutive day's journey, and the pony could really hardly drag one leg after another: the hard soil seemed more fatiguing to the animal than the previous sand.

Our tents were pitched considerably out of the road, for security against Hadji travellers, (or robbers,) and we could only discover it by the intervention of fire-arms, for the evening closed in so suddenly with rain, that we only traced Denino by his firing off his pistols, and then his gun, to attract our attention. He had contrived, in giving us this notice, to shoot into a covey of partridges, which added a very dry and tasteless dish to our bill of fare.

Our supplies from Suez had been limited,

as we were told, that at the station-house*
we should meet with *all the delicacies of the
season*, but one turkey and a gigantic cauliflower was all that could be found, as it
seems that a Christian party, as they described it, had arrived from Cairo, to make
their *beiram* in the Desert, and had eat up
everything.   I suppose the want of change
of scene and customs must be greatly felt at
Cairo, when Europeans could find it a party
of pleasure to come a long day's journey
into the Desert, in such bad weather too, to
eat their Christmas dinner.

The computation of the distance from

* At this station Mr. Hill, proprietor of an hotel at
Cairo, has built a considerable inn.   There are four
other station-houses, beside the principal one, on the
Desert, and Mr. Hill's public spirit may be conceived
from the fact, that he had to carry all his materials,
even the water with which to make the mortar, either
from Suez or the Nile.   In this inn there are a dozen
good bed-rooms, and at the other stations, sufficient
accommodation for a moderate party.

Cairo is so contradictory, that one does not know whom to believe. It is, however, a consolation to feel that we are in reality approaching the end of our journey, as the distance cannot now be above thirty miles.

We read the Evening Service, and I think Divine worship in a tent, in the Desert, must a good deal approach to the impressiveness of what I have so often heard described at sea.

We met, during this day's journey, many Hadjis, chiefly from Morocco, wearing immense broad-brimmed straw hats, resembling umbrellas. Some of these poor pilgrims were so anxious to obtain a drop of water, that they came up to us, and endeavoured to ascertain, by thrusting their spears into our baggage, whether we had any. George and the Cavasse drew up, pointed their guns, and prevented further aggression.

DECEMBER 30TH.—We arrived at the last station about two, and then found donkey-chairs, horses, and luncheon, sent out by Mr. Waghorn, to meet us. It was a great relief to find shelter, after a long ride, against cutting wind and dust, which I think must have been of the sharp quality, engendering ophthalmia.

The donkey-chairs are perfectly charming, consisting of an easy arm-chair, fixed on a board like a dinner-tray, with poles slung on two donkeys, one before, and the other behind, in short, occupying the place of sedan-chairmen, but with infinitely more steadiness and activity. Their action is a sort of amble, and the smoothest manner of progress I ever experienced. A boy is in attendance on each equipage, who runs by the side of the chair, which will proceed, without apparent fatigue to boy or beast, at least six miles an hour.

The city of Cairo, which is said to contain 350,000 souls, appears perfectly immense at the first view, which it presents at the abrupt termination of the Desert, and the effect of the extreme verdure of the borders of the Nile appeared almost dazzling, before it became refreshing, so bright is the character of the vegetation, (at least at this season) independently of the contrast it afforded, after fifteen days passed in a sandy region, including Suez, where not a trace of vegetation could be seen. The Caliphs' tombs were our first architectural objects.

We were very much disappointed at the pyramids not rising in gigantic grandeur before us, as we had so completely anticipated. They were not, in fact, to be seen from this approach.

The portion of the bazaar and streets we threaded on our way to the hotel, were much more striking and picturesque than any we had seen at Constantinople; in fact, they should not be compared. Then the streets are unpaved, and, considering the denseness of the population and their general absence of cleanliness, they are in wonderfully good condition. The upper stories of the houses all but touch, and the carved and painted latticed windows present the most Moorish effect, and realize one's notion of Spanish decoration, being, I suppose, its primitive character.

How our humble donkeys and ourselves escaped annihilation from the highly loaded and gigantic race of camels, which passed us in all directions, I cannot imagine, particularly as the general din of the camel conductors removed any single or distinct order of precedence.

Our attention was so attracted towards our means of escape, through the activities of our attendant *imps*, that it quite secured us against alarm. Not so an elderly English lady, whom we met riding with, we supposed, her two daughters. She appeared the re-animated illustration of Theodore Hook's celebrated Mrs. Lavinia Ramsbottom. She was seated on a very tiny donkey, *en grande toilette*, her bonnet and cloak of enormous dimensions; the latter was of very glaring colours, and so completely covering the donkey, that only his head and tail could be distinguished.　The old lady looked as if she were swimming, attended by a tall turbaned Turk, who held his arm tight round her waist to support her, and who, in consequence of this exertion, leaned himself against the nearly invisible donkey.

The whole progress seemed to be achieved by machinery, and the effect was so ludicrous, that, in spite of my attempt to be decorous, I actually laughed in my countrywoman's face; but her fears occupied her too much for us to dread her resentment.

The younger ladies, attended by some European beaus, were too animated and occupied in purchases at a grocer's stall, to remark my ill-breeding.　I suppose the party must be on their way to India, for they did not look as if travelling for pleasure or antiquities.

Apropos to ignorance—on leaving our last encampment, we found strewed on the road several pieces of what appeared to be logs of wood, and we regretted not having been able to appropriate them for our kitchen fire, where fuel had proved so scarce. On closer examination, however, we found them to be all petrifactions, and of so perfect a character, that even the splinters were solidly *attached and detached*, and these *bûches* (for they appeared exactly like those prepared for a good French fire) had so completely the appearance of light and dry wood, that only on lifting them (which was a matter of difficulty) could one be convinced of the fact of their being solid stone, and of greater weight than the size justified, as if partly of metal. We are quite anxious to have our dark minds illuminated on the subject.

We found in the Frank quarter very tolerably comfortable rooms, at the hotel kept by Mr. Waghorn's brother-in-law. Mr. Waghorn himself had just arrived from Alexandria, but did not bring any news later than what we had read at Suez. He seemed to engage heart and soul in forwarding rapidity of conveyance to India. He deserves great credit for what he has already achieved.

The voyage from England to Bombay can now be performed in thirty-seven days. Mr. W. asserts, that it was Mr. Pitt's opinion, that when England could communicate with India and receive a reply in the course of eight months, then, and not till then, might she think of changing her system of government, and that what he (Mr. W.) was considered as a visionary for attempting but a few years before, is now more than realized.

Mehemet Ali has greatly imbued him with

his own opinion, both of his resources and stupendous influence, and of his power of raising a million of Arab soldiers, to fight his battles. This at least is in strong contradiction to what we heard in Turkey and Syria, but I believe there is no doubt of the degree of national pride the Egyptian Arabs entertain, with regard to the splendour and consequence of Cairo. The improvements Mehemet Ali is conducting may tell more than is suspected on the general mass of the people.

The comfort of arriving at this end of our journey is greatly diminished, from finding none of the letters we were most anxious to receive.

DECEMBER 31ST.—We set off on our donkeys, after a most noisy struggle among the donkey-boys, candidates for our selection. The little by-street in which our hotel stood was, unluckily for us, one of the chief stations, and we had the *too* great choice of

at least fifty of these little animals and their
conductors, screaming in Italian and particularly good English, their individual recom-
mendations,—" My good donkey, my lady!
he go ten miles hour!"—"My donkey little
race-horse!" &c. &c.

Some of the boys' dresses were so picturesque, from their wearing tunics of deep
blue linen; the loose sleeves, and sometimes the drapery was confined by a scarlet
cord: the combination produced so much the
effect of Raphael's and Correggio's colouring.

I never before experienced the perfection
of smooth progressive motion. The fleetness
of the Egyptian asses' amble is not to be
described : one glides on, and, as on a
rail-road, you only can judge of the rapidity
of your progress by seeing how fast you lose
sight of succeeding objects. I am longing
to take some to England. What charming
shooting ponies they would make ! if I may
be permitted the Hibernicism. The race

is quite a thing apart : their coats are so fine, that when clipped they look as if they were dressed in grey or white satin, for some are nearly colourless.

The Egyptian mules are beautiful animals, and seem to be as much in use among the officers and richer classes as horses. A handsome one cannot be had for less than 50*l*.

We first passed the mosque of the Sultan Hassan, of the Saracenic order of architecture. It is very lofty and striking, however incorrect in style it is considered. The entrance-door is of great height, and indeed disproportioned to the general elevation. The depth consists of a series of arches very deeply sculptured in Arabesque designs, and light columns formed by twisted snakes. The whole mosque was very highly, and in some parts elaborately ornamented, and greatly surpassed in beauty the smooth whitewashed walls and minarets of the Constantinople mosques.

This part of Cairo is comparatively modern. It leads to the citadel, which is looked upon as the original fortress, and is partly cut in the rock, while the remainder includes portions of Roman, Saracenic, and Egyptian architecture.   We mounted a steep and slippery ascent, and passed through the very gates of the citadel which, in 1812, were shut upon the unfortunate Mamelukes, who were inclosed in the court of the fortress, and fired upon by its guns :   about five hundred were massacred on the spot.

One alone escaped : he contrived to reach the battlement of the tower on horseback, assisted by treading on the mass of the slain ; from this point, a height of sixty feet, he made his leap.   His horse was killed on the spot, and he, though severely wounded, contrived to drag himself for some distance to the confines of the Desert, from whence he made his escape.

This fact is otherwise described in Russell's life of Mehemet Ali. It is there stated that he arrived the last, and was shut out of the citadel; but Sir F. Henniker was in Cairo at the time, and what I have mentioned above was described to Sir F. H. by a spectator. *C'est le succès qui couronne l'œuvre.* This very Hanim Bey now governs one of the Syrian pachalics under Mehemet Ali's authority.

The view from the court of Yousouff (Joseph) adjoining the citadel is quite splendid, and so extensive, that the pyramids, fifteen miles off, did not appear to be half the distance that the eye could have reached. The mention of Joseph's hall sounded very interesting, but one was soon called back from the patriarchal times, to which one's ideas had travelled, to the fact that this Joseph was the vizier of the Sultan Saladin, and the founder of the most celebrated institutions of his reign. Some columns of granite standing near this spot are quite of colossal proportions.

The court was a few years ago nearly destroyed by the explosion of the powder magazine. The fragments of pillars, eight yards in diameter, scattered about, prove the awful combustion which must have taken place. Since this period the magazine has been transferred six miles from the city.

Mehemet Ali has lately commenced the building of a new mosque, of which we were shewn the foundation and superstructure. It will be finer (if ever finished) than any existing in Cairo, built of beautifully clear marble, very much of the character of what we call Egyptian alabaster, but its frequent flaws require the insertion of stucco and cement. The quarry from which it is taken has only been opened three years, and the polished brilliancy of the marble will make it very remarkable.

We next visited a new palace of the vice-roy, with some very handsome, but vulgarly furnished apartments; the taste, alas! of

an English upholsterer! The garden surrounding it is very pretty. The palace
communicates with many of the public
offices : about six hundred *employés* are
lodged in the precincts.

We were shewn the Hall of Proclamations,
where, no later than a few weeks ago, the
farce of reading the young Sultan's late
hatti scheriff took place. In the adjoining
Court of Requests, we were informed, that
at four P. M. bastinado and other kinds of
punishment took place, and that we were at
liberty to remain there and witness any of the
proceedings that could give us gratification.
This liberal permission we declined, which
seemed rather to surprise the Master of the
Ceremonies.

We made a *détour* to visit the mosque
of Amurath. We returned to our hotel,
where we found some crazy-looking English
carriages, in waiting to convey us to the
garden of Schoubra, a distance of about

a league, through an avenue of fine acacias, which in this climate are trees of considerable size, and afforded us delightful shade from the glare and dust. The pods of these acacias are of the size of tamarinds. I never saw anything to be compared to the beauty of the Schoubra garden. It is quite an illustration of those described in the Arabian nights. It is formed in the original Grecian plan of garden : straight rows, but thickly planted, and covering three square miles in extent. The lemon, orange, myrtle, and pomegranate succeeded to and touched each other, and below these, hedges of geranium in bright and full flower ; the whole garden appeared to have been just watered, and produced the most refreshing and yet not overpowering fragrance.

We felt quite revived and enchanted, and might be excused for our constant and repeated terms of admiration, of " Oh ! how sweet !—Oh ! how charming !" Tired as I

was on arriving, I soon felt quite restored
with the effect of so balmy an atmosphere.
We were shewn a kiosk, not yet completed,
of beautiful construction, and the *beau idéal*
of what would be calculated for an Eastern
fête. The gallery occupied the sides of a
square filled with water, in the centre of
which is a marble fountain, which you reach
by flights of steps, surrounded by some
extent of pavement, inclosed by a balustrade, and in short affording dry ground for
several hundred people, (such a station for
an orchestra !) and leaving space in the wide
galleries for walking and supping; and,
indeed, the four corners of the square would
afford as many ball-rooms, as they are di-
vided off in oblique compartments. But
what can be the object of this beautiful
erection, in which a fête to five thousand
persons could be given, in a country where
the inhabitants neither habitually dance,
sing, sup, nor *socialize?*

H 3

We were obliged to hurry home, as the
gates close at sunset.   The quick running
of the reis, or attendant Arabs, was quite
distressing to us, but evidently not to them,
though they kept up with the carriages as
they drove at very quick speed for at least
forty minutes.

We only stopped once, to see the arrival
of two Indian passengers, in the shape of
elephants, intended as presents to Mehemet
Ali.   This incident quite gave us a glance
of India, particularly as we were told by
some of the party, who were just arrived
from Calcutta, that at this point of the road
the vegetation had a good deal of the character of the jungle verdure.   The Hindos-
tanee conductors made their elephants go
through various manœuvres with great good
humour.   They had such agreeable and
open expression of countenance ; and one
felt struck by their superiority in that
respect, contrasted with the Arabs.

We hurried over our dinner, to prepare for the magician's visit, which we thought appropriate to a new year's eve. Our necromancer, however, had neither a fine nor prepossessing countenance. He began his operations in the way described by Lane and other travellers—writing on slips of paper, which he rolled up and consumed in a charcoal brazier, muttering a kind of incantation.

The *victim* was an Arab boy belonging to the hotel, who had the ink rubbed on his palm, and was desired to describe all he saw reflected in it; he began, as is always the case, to say he saw colours flying, a camp, the Sultan's flag, and men sweeping. I suspect this boy will never again be selected, as he did not prove at all a good coadjutor. There never was such a failure; for we gave him great latitude, and asked for the queen, whom he described as a tall woman holding a *shamsee* (parasol), and wearing a man's hat. We tried to persuade ourselves it was broad daylight at Windsor, at that moment, that the parasol was a whip, and the hat a riding one.

We then asked for Lord Fitzroy Somerset. He was described with both arms, and as being thirty. Sir Henry Hardinge we also tried, and failed. Sir Frederic Adams was described with yellow hair, and about forty. In short, our friend, Mr. Edward Jerningham was the only redeeming point of the exhibition; he was described as dark, tall, handsome, and with his hair very short— twirling a stick with one hand, and the other laid on his breast. Now, as he had been wounded at the Eglintoun tournament, and had been condemned to have his head shaved and his arm confined for weeks in a sling, a little imagination served to make this description admissible.

I was very glad that my usual credulity and superstition were rather diminished than increased by this exhibition, and extreme absurdity of the whole proceeding. I think the magician must have read in our countenances the entire failure of his *supernatural* efforts.

Just as he had taken his departure, we were attracted to the window by a jingling noise, like that by which bees are drawn to their hives. This proved the precursor of a native band of kettle-drums. Immediately we saw a very prettily-dressed procession pass, the lights well arranged; in short, the well-organized ceremony of a betrothal. The parties, a little boy and girl of six years old, were mounted on fine caparisoned horses, supported by people on each side holding perfumed handkerchiefs to their noses. The children were beautifully dressed, and of the highest class; their marriage will not take place for six years to come. There are frequent instances of betrothal at even an earlier age than this.

Poor little things ! one quite lamented their being kept out of their beds and paraded at this late, cold hour.

I retired to rest, perfectly giddy and tired with the variety of things I had seen and done during the last twelve hours.

CHAPTER IX.

JANUARY 1st, 1840.—We began the new year with an expedition to Boulac, for the purpose of securing a good boat for our voyage to Thebes; the day cold and dusty, very much reminding one of a March day at Brighton. In consequence of the viceroy having laid an embargo on all the flat-bottomed boats, for the purpose of transporting his grain, we had a very scanty choice; but we were assured that to English foreigners this monopoly would not apply, and that in a few days our boats from Alexandria would arrive, or some be supplied from Cairo.

I had heard so much of the capacious size and luxury with which boats could be prepared for the Nile expedition, I confess I was disappointed at finding the cabin of such narrow proportions, that only two people could possibly be in it at once; and that Minney and Christine must either be suffocated in the inner cabin, or sleep on the deck with merely an awning, which this season did not justify, and that at the least two of the largest boats would be required.

The usual habit of packing on what are considered parties of pleasure (and these of six weeks' duration!) in the smallest possible compass, made it impossible for me to find any one disposed to listen to my murmuring observations about ill-closed windows—confined space, &c. Every inconvenience I remarked upon was passed over as a matter of course, or by assurances of the excellence of the crew, and congratulations on the coldness of the season having destroyed all *animal matter*. I found George quite blinded on the subject, by the specious pleading of our conductors, and for the sake of the beauty and interest of our journey into Upper Egypt, becoming of most " *squeezable materials*" on all points connected with our proposed expedition.

This first view of the Nile rather diminished my ideas of its magnificence. One is obliged to consider its usefulness, and overlook its unpicturesque appearance; which is a hard trial with regard to a new acquaintance.

Although our boat-hunting consumed a great deal of time and patience, we determined it should not prevent us, when so near, from going to see the English garden at Rhoda, reported to be the site of the spot where Moses was adopted by Pharaoh's daughter. The original garden of Rhoda was said to have been made, centuries back, by a caliph, for his favourite sultana, who pined for her beautiful and fertile country in some Greek settlement, and this garden was constructed to meet her wishes and remind her of her native soil ; in short, a very fanciful and pretty story is told respecting it. But the original garden has for many centuries become a perfect sand-bank, and only two trees (the sycamore ficus) stood to attest its former position. For the object of employing idle hands, Mehemet Ali, twelve years ago, determined to restore it, in spite of every natural obstacle, and he has so perfectly succeeded that the garden, unlike the one at Schoubra, already pays its own expenses.

It is very pretty, but to my unscientific eyes is very inferior to the one just mentioned. An Irish and a Scotch gardener are associated in the superintendence of this botanical garden, and it will be the nursery garden of all Egypt. Mehemet Ali has sent the Irish gardener, M'Cullen, both to India and Mexico to collect plants, and all appear to thrive,—bananas, teak, guavas, cocoanuts, pines, caoutchouc, &c. Trees of only ten years' growth must have been at least thirty feet high.

This territory is considered as Ibrahim Pacha's property, and his harem opens into its grounds ; they inclose a grotto, composed of shells found on the shore of the Red Sea, and arranged with great taste. The entrance is very narrow, but there is sufficient space for the sociable smoking parties in which Ibrahim is said to indulge greatly. In the centre of the grotto is a crystal fountain rushing into a marble basin, which must give most refreshing coolness in the hot season, which Ibrahim Pacha says is only supportable in this spot.

We found dining in our private room so difficult an undertaking, and so unusual a proceeding, that we resigned ourselves to the table d'hôte, where we made acquaintance with several interesting travellers from the " far East."

We went afterwards to a little theatre, half amateur, half artiste, where they were acting a little Italian vaudeville. The prettiest part of the *spectacle* was the audience, which almost entirely consisted of ladies in the Levantine costume, which from its variety and richness is very peculiar. The greatest proportion of the young and pretty women were Jewesses. Some of their head-dresses were magnificent in point of diamond ornaments, and their hair plaited in perhaps twenty tresses hanging down their backs, and so thickly studded with gold coins, that it looked like chain armour, and would, I think, resist a sabre cut.

An hour's theatrical attendance satisfied my curiosity, and I came home to find in our court a very merry and noisy party of camel-drivers and donkey-boys, to whom Mr. Waghorn had given a New Year's feast. Their dancing and singing resembled those of the most savage tribe, at least so an American traveller told us, who had been a good deal with the North American Indians. One, however, danced very gracefully, with a scarf he formed by unrolling his turban, and in a manner reminding one so much of the Spanish dancing, and probably of this its Moorish origin.

JANUARY 2ND.—The day so windy and disagreeable, that I did not accompany *my belongings* on their expedition to the great plain, from whence the pilgrims started in some thousands for Mecca. I was assured I had missed a very pretty and characteristic scene. The din of marriage-processions is become quite intolerable. I believe our quarters must be the Little Maddox-street of Cairo.

JANUARY 3RD.—We took an interesting ride to the tombs of the Caliphs and Mameluke kings, which are highly picturesque and very magnificent, but fast falling to decay, though by the commonest repair their architectural beauty might so well be preserved. Mehemet Ali has provided himself with a most comfortable family sepulchre, not far from this quarter, consisting of three dry, warm, well-carpeted apartments; the only comfortable rooms I have found at Cairo: there are at least thirty monuments in them, dedicated to his brothers, nieces, and grandchildren.

On our return we made a circuit by the citadel, to see the beautiful effect of the setting sun sinking behind the Pyramids.

JANUARY 4TH.—We were invited by Dr. Abbott, to visit the library he is endeavouring to establish at Cairo, and take the chance of finding an interesting mummy. Among the several mummy-cases he proposed opening, he chose the most promising, but it was by no means an interesting *subject,* as no ornaments were found underneath the cerecloth by which it was enveloped ; the hands and feet were gilt, and by the smallness of their proportions it was supposed to be the mummy of a lady of fashion. The process of the examination I did not think agreeable. One felt the hardship attending the fair Egyptian's fate, that after having for three thousand years secured her *incognita*, all these precautions should have been destroyed by our idle, unscientific curiosity.

Dr. Abbott joined our dinner party, and proved a very agreeable *convive.* Our vice-consul was living in the country, the gentleman for whom Sir G. Wilkinson had given us a letter of introduction was absent, and Colonel Vyse and Signor Caviglia had also flitted, so that we had been obliged to let our *lionizing* entirely depend upon our books of travels, and frequently on our donkey-boys. We greatly felt the absence of a *point d'appui*, having hitherto been particularly indulged by friendly *Ciceronisme*.

Father and daughter undertook a long ride towards the Suez desert, to see the beginning of the Petrified Forest, about which so little is heard, though an object of great interest. One piece of the timber (if it may be so called) consisted of a single trunk, which although broken was not separated, and measured ninety feet in length.

The general features of the country at this point, from the outline of the distant mountains, are very picturesque. Poor Mons. Chacaton's ague proved a most inconvenient visiter at Cairo, where every street and corner offers such beautiful shadows and subjects for the pencil. Our doctor found here two of his countrymen and fraternity, and as there is a great deal of sickness, and little or no pay, they associate him very cordially in their practice.

JANUARY 5TH.—We traversed the principal square and quarter of Cairo, to attend the English service, which is admirably performed by the German missionaries. The principal one, Mr. Lieder, has fitted up by far the nicest Protestant chapel we have met with abroad. The sermon, preached by Mr. Crozier, also a German, was an excellently comprehensive discourse, referring in an interesting manner to the periods of the religious history of Egypt. The perseverance of some of the principal missionaries, in acquiring the Coptic language, and in establishing schools, and in reforming the gross errors that have gradually deformed the original Christian creed, is likely to tell on the next generation, as the young Copts shew great aptitude in acquiring knowledge, and are very zealous in communicating instruction to their parents, who are becoming very proud of their progeny's erudition. A Protestant service in the Coptic language is regularly performed.

The language, from having become much corrupted, is very difficult to acquire. There is, probably, only one European woman in existence acquainted with it, Miss Tatham, who had assisted her father in his religious duties, and from the habit of transcribing gradually acquired the language. She is described as unassuming as she is intelligent, and was of great assistance by giving religious instruction in the Coptic female schools.

We dined with Dr. Abbott, completely *à la Turque*, no chairs, knives or forks, each presented with a wooden spoon, and the dinner spread on a large round tray, placed on a table not larger than a footstool, and about a foot and half from the ground ; only one dish was served at a time, from which the host first takes a *thumb and finger full*, the spoon being only used for the smofa (soup) and rice-milk.

We had a succession of at least fourteen dishes, though we were only six *entertained*. Some of the compositions were excellent, but the predominance of grease and acids must make them dreadfully unwholesome. The meat is so completely boiled to rags, it could afford no sort of nourishment. I am only surprised at the Turks being in such generally good condition, for a thin one is seldom to be seen.

Minney and I went home on our donkeys, which conveyance supersedes all others in comfort in these regions. The gentlemen adjourned to a genuine Turkish party, to which they were invited to see the Almée dancing, which Mehemet Ali, in his decorous spirit of reform, is discouraging as much as possible. I suppose the beauty of this style of dancing, as well as that of the Bayadères we had seen the year before at Paris, was much exaggerated, for they returned home much more tired than pleased by the exhibition.

JANUARY 6TH.—We began our day with a visit to Dr. Abbott, that we might see by daylight his small, but interesting collection of antiquities. He has some specimens of Saracenic arms, which, in the eyes of connoisseurs, are beautiful, and some mummies, which he had despoiled of some gold ornaments of beautiful workmanship.

I very much coveted one, about the size and shape of a *ferronière*, a winged orb, the well-known emblem of immortality, the representation of which is so constantly met with on the Egyptian tombs. This ornament was a little broken, but of the purest and brightest gold. The wings were beautifully enamelled, or rather varied in colour, by the insertion of lapis lazuli and

a reddish stone. I think such minute execution would shame Storr and Mortimer.
I am surprised they have not already been
imitated, the form is so singularly *elegant !*
I cannot find any other term by which to
express their beauty.

We rode on to the Mauristan and slave-
market, which, though picturesque in elevation, are very disagreeable objects, as the
Mauristan is the most dreadful picture of a
mad-house that can be imagined. I was not
the least aware of its character till I saw
cages round a court, like those of an ill-kept
menagerie; in these, melancholy, for they
were not noisy, mad people, were incarce-
rated. The fee exacted is at least a rea-
sonable one : you are obliged to purchase
a certain quantity of bread for these poor
maniacs, which is provided for that purpose,
at the entrance gate of the Mauristan.

We had, from not knowing the way
effected our entrance through a beautiful

mosque, and the absence of the *faithful*, and our ignorance, had served us better than patronage, in seeing this beautiful specimen of Moorish architecture.

Our afternoon expedition was under the auspices of Signora N——, a Levantine interpretess, and was arranged to visit the harem of Halib Effendi, the ex-governor of Cairo. We were joined by three Miss G——'s, amiable Irish ladies, who had, with their brother, been seven years on their travels, reserving London, where they had never been, for their later lion. The staircase and entrance of the house were much like those in France and Italy.

We passed two black slaves richly dressed. A heavily embroidered curtain being put aside, we found ourselves in a large apartment, with no furniture, except the ever-to-be-met-with divan, extending round the three sides of the room. The lady who received us was a rara-avis, a sort of Turkish chanoinesse, an unmarried daughter of the Effendi's, of thirty-two years of age. She was so like Lady C——y, and Lady A. F—x, that I almost expected her to speak to me in English.

Her dress looked like a riding-habit, being a tight blue cloth jacket, with a coloured neckcloth, and her hair cut straight round her forehead, with a sort of black cap or turban at the back of her head. It was only when she got up and displayed a long train and a diamond comb, that her dress became a little more feminine. She had a most agreeable and intelligent countenance, and appeared intended for something very superior to her condition.

She took us to a room in which a quantity of silk-worms were being reared, and where a perfect manufactory of raw silk was preparing; she took me a little apart, and unlocked a drawer, from which she produced some paintings of flowers, copied from an

English Ackermann, and really tolerably done. My approbation encouraged her to shew me a copy-book, like those used at our infant schools, and a very tattered Télémaque, and though she professed to know no European language, it was evident she was trying to educate herself. She shewed us a French grammar and dictionary, which she told us had belonged to a brother she had lost, and who had been in Paris and London.

All her companions, including her mother, (for whose society she had renounced marriage,) looked like inferior beings; one really longed to assist her in emancipating herself from the thraldom of ignorance and superstition, not indeed that she looked unhappy, but had an air of energy and intelligence in all she said or did, that would have been remarkable under any circumstances.

She looked at my bracelet, containing the children's hair, and, asking me if they were all alive, returned it to me in a graceful manner, saying, "May God preserve them to you!"

She told us she would go down the Nile with us, and learn English, if we would leave our husbands and brothers at Cairo, and seemed highly diverted at the notion of such an *escapade*.

I was very much struck with the beauty of one of the slaves, who brought in coffee and sherbet; she was a Circassian, and, I should think, the very perfection of height and proportion: she had a fair, clear, and beautiful texture of skin, with a mild and dignified expression of countenance, to which it is impossible, by description, to do justice; in regularity and cast of features, a good deal resembling the late Mrs. Arbuthnot.

She wore a yellow turban, and a partial drapery of the deep blue of a Raphael picture; her arms were of beautiful form, and crossed, resting on the shawl folded round her waist, which gave her the classical *pose*

I 3

one sees in antique sculpture, and which so few European artists have the good fortune to copy. I never so much wished to draw, and be able thus to convey this *beau ideal* of female refined beauty. She did not at all appear conscious that she represented it, but our interpretess told us she had always been remarked by whatever European lady visitors this harem had received, but the chiefs had never appreciated the merit of the selection.

On our return to our hotel, we found the prospects of our expedition to Thebes much deranged, by the arrival of newspapers, announcing the meeting of parliament a month earlier was expected. I received this intelligence with a great mixture of feeling; I rather believe, the prospect of getting home some six weeks earlier predominated.

It was proposed to me that we should join Mrs. Leider's party, to visit Princess Nazly Hanim, Mehemet Ali's favourite daughter, to present her with a print of the Queen, which she expressed a wish to have, as a return for some civility and service she had procured for the Missionary Society, whose female members are much encouraged to visit the harems at Cairo, and no resistance made to their entering on the discussion of religious matters, which argues in favour of Mehemet Ali's religious tolerance.

This Princess Nazly is a widow of forty-five: her late husband, Deftudgus Bey, was supposed to have been the most cruel of men, and to have caused more bloodshed than any man of his time. His widow is thought to have shared in this propensity, and if half is true that is told of her, she must be a terrible princess indeed. It is said that a young Greek slave, a few weeks ago, accidentally burnt some article of this illustrious lady's dress, and that the punishment inflicted upon her was so severe, that she made her escape, and took refuge at the Greek consul's, from whence he was induced, by the princess's fair promises and influence, to give her up, after three days' protection. This cruel compliance was followed up by the poor girl being shut up, and, as is said, by a joint of one of her fingers being daily amputated from the hand that caused the accident, and this as a commutation of punishment, however Colonel C—— and other authorities dispute this scandal.

The Turks are very anxious for European medical advice, but reverse the general habit of fees ; and on one occasion Dr. A——, after long attendance, and ultimate cure, was asked for *backshish*. Inquiring under what pretence, he was told, to pay for so much valuable experience : he is frequently allowed to attend the ladies.

One consulted him for what was palpitation of the heart, and he was desired to call again. On his following visit, he was told that a consultation of the principal doctresses had taken place, and that they perfectly agreed with him, that the nature of the complaint was an affection of the heart, and that, to get it back into its right place, they were just in the act of tying her up by the feet, which would produce the proper effect of re-establishing it in its position.

CHAPTER X.

Cross the Nile—Giza—Ascent of a pyramid—Monument of Cheops—The king's chamber—English
inscriptions—The tomb of Numbers—Visit to the
Sphinxes—Sacrilegious fuel—Pyramids of Dashour—Bird mummy-pits—The Reis of Saqquarha
—Strange contents of a packet from England.

JANUARY 7TH.—We determined upon our
expedition to the Pyramids, and renewing
our Desert encampment in preference to
sleeping in the tombs, which is the general
resource when the visitors to the Pyramids
do not return to sleep at Cairo.

Dr. A——— and Mr. E——— having joined
our party, we crossed the Nile, at what is

called Old Cairo, about two hours' ride distant. The bustle of embarking our camels and donkeys was very great, and the general effect most picturesque, from the variety of the Nile boats on the river, the Pyramids forming the back-ground. I regretted that the daylight was so short, as not to allow Mons. Chacaton to make a drawing from this point, as, at the Pyramids themselves, it is next to impossible.

We reached Giza at four, and had time to arrange our tents, before we ascended the Pyramids to see the sun set. I cannot imagine how we so easily gained the summit, which is four hundred and sixty feet from the sand. Instead of the Pyramid presenting a flat surface, as I imagined, from the effect at a distance, they would do, large stones of thirty feet long, and none less than five high, are placed at the back of each other, in a *pyramidical* form. The stepping from one stone to another, without support

of any kind, is achieved by the assistance
and activity of the Arab conductors, who, by
dragging, pushing, and their animated cries,
contrive to get you up, in spite of your
wasting energies.

I ascended the last, having the assistance
of *six arms* to my share, and, looking up at
my *predecessors*, I was reminded of a French
mythological ballet, where Psyche and other
characters are seen dragged by the furies.
Minney appeared to fly up the Pyramids,
and her arms looked as if they would be
drawn out of their sockets by her two wild
Arab attendants. She was closely followed
by Christine, her father, and the doctor,
the latter of whom did not appear to fly, but
presented the image of a pinioned criminal
on the rack. The whole effect was so ridi-
culous, as sadly to diminish our expectations of the sublime. The ascent only employed us a quarter of an hour. We only
rested twice on our way, which was as

necessary for our guides' lungs as our own.

The view of course is very extensive, embracing Cairo and the whole range of the scattered Pyramids. The sunset was not a brilliant one, and we all doubted whether our powers would allow us to repeat our exertions the next morning, to see the sun rise, the usual duty of conscientious travellers. We found the repetition of our Desert fare, and even our tent beds, much superior to our hotel accommodation, or perhaps we felt more *at home.*

JANUARY 8TH.—The weather was so fine, and our encampment so comfortable, that we determined on remaining two days longer in the neighbourhood of the Pyramids, and set off after breakfast to visit the monument of Cheops. The entrance is not quite in the centre, and only three and a half feet high. The necessity of a continued stooping position, as we alternately mounted and descended during a distance of several hundred feet, was exceedingly fatiguing. The renewed assistance of my *trio*, Hanim, Hassan, and Mahomet, was not nearly as effectual as when I was climbing a continued ascent, and I began to think my preceding day's feat perfect repose in comparison to the exhaustion, the suffocating heat, and dust, attending my present exploit.

The king's chamber, as it is called, the object of our toil, enjoyed a somewhat cooler atmosphere. It is merely a vaulted chamber, containing a red granite sarcophagus, measuring seven feet four inches by three feet six inches; another chamber is called Lady Arbuthnot's, as she was the first lady who penetrated into it. Among the names preserved on its walls, in which the Smiths and Jacksons remarkably predominated, I did not see more than half-a-dozen ladies' names—five English !

We were here joined by a party dressed so completely *à l'Orientale*, that my attention was drawn by the decoration of the *legion d'honneur*, to the consideration of the country of the leader, whom we found to be Mons. Coombes, a pleasing and intelligent Frenchman, who had been thus *decoré* on account of his work on Abyssinian antiquities. He was on his road into Abyssinia to pursue his researches still further.

We next visited the Tomb of Numbers, so called I believe from its containing tables connected with the early commerce of Egypt. This we were obliged to enter, not on our hands and knees, but as if we were swimming, so very low is the entrance. Fortunately this exertion only continued for the distance of a few yards. The tomb itself is ornamented by the representations of animals, chiefly cows and calves. Some were beautifully

executed, with the colouring quite preserved.

We came out perfectly covered with very
fine dust. Our hair looked as if it had been
powdered, and our garments were in shreds,
from our constant collision with the stones.
The doctor was in a sad plight, because his
best coat had in one' hour become his worst.
His regard for future fame, at Vienna, had
spurred him to an undertaking not at all
suitable to his natural disposition, and his
heart was at Cairo, where he was much
mixed up in the medical dispute of pro and
anti plague contagionists.

We finished this most fatiguing morning's
sight-seeing by a visit to the Sphinx. She
has again modestly imbedded herself in the
sand, and all Colonel Vyse's labour and ex-
pense have proved as transitory as the result
produced by the attempts of the French
in 1799.

We were about three hours reaching the

Pyramids of Saqquarda; the latter part of the road was through a primitive village desert burial ground, thickly planted with date-trees. Some of these clumps were *fait à peindre*; and our artist's tertian ague came very inconveniently, as we were suddenly met by two unveiled Arabian women, who had not time to hide their really beautiful countenances.

We found Denino very forward in his cooking, comfortably encamped close to some water, which seemed full of wild geese and ducks, quite at hand for second course, but our doctor would not hear of so marshy a position, and we were obliged to remove, much to the discomfiture of our attendants. The wood they gathered was so green we could not succeed in making a good fire, till we discovered the outer case of a mummy coffin, which had probably been flung aside by some late amateur excavator. This well-preserved wood made us most excellent, however sacrilegious fuel.

Of our many busy days of sight-seeing, I think this had been the most fatiguing.

JANUARY 9TH.—The heat of the day was so intense, I had not courage to proceed, with my *belongings*, to the Pyramids of Dashour, two hours distant. The peculiarity of these is, that they are built of unburnt bricks. Discoveries may still remain to be made in the principal and yet unopened pyramid. On the return of my party they visited the Bird mummy-pits ; but these proving too deep for Minney to be let down into, they brought back some jars as an *echantillon*.

We found, on opening one, some rather large bones, which Dr. A—— conjectured to be those of an ibis. They were swathed by strips of cloth, in the same manner as the human mummies. The colours and texture of the feathers were quite distinct, but the covering of bitumen being removed, they fell to pieces on being touched.

The evening towards sunset was so fine, that I joined the second expedition, in visiting a tomb opened by Mr. Caviglia, about seven years before, called that of Psammeticus or Rameses II. It is of beautiful form and proportions, containing paintings and well-engraven hieroglyphics. It is more interesting and less difficult of entrance than the tomb of Numbers at Giza. I am surprised that it is not more celebrated; for its very existence was only casually mentioned to us by the Reiz of Saqquarda, who was sitting for his picture to Minney and Mr. E——ds.

His dress was far more picturesque than his countenance, but such was not his own opinion, for he repeatedly and conceitedly regretted not having sat for his portrait when he was in possession of his fine teeth. He explained their absence, by saying that he had knocked out his front teeth to avoid conscription, as soldiers are thus rendered unable to fulfil the necessary obligation of biting their cartridges. This Reiz was the only exception we met with to the simplicity of the Arabs, and their indifference to personal advantages. Our doctor had returned to Cairo in the morning, to look after our letters, as the Maltese mail was again due; and just as we got home a man arrived with a very promising packet, countersigned by Mr. Walne, the vice-consul. Great was our pleasure, and almost greater our disappointment at finding the contents of the packet merely a few London bills, and half a dozen letters from different writers, all to the same purport, asking George, in varied and civil phraseology, to afford his autograph, in the way of frank, to perfect his or her collection, just when franking was about to be abolished, and the new system of postage commenced:

To receive London bills and requests for franks at the Pyramids would have been laughable enough had not our anxiety for *home* letters been so earnest.

CHAPTER XI.

The site of Memphis—Statue of Sesostris—Real anti-
quities—Rich soil—The inhabitants—Vultures—
Fresh arrivals—Visit to a Turkish bath—The
Princess's palace—Shami Bey's harem—The fair
Saramé—Our entertainment—Feasting—Dancing
and singing.

JANUARY 10TH.—Prepared to leave our
encampment with much regret, feeling it
would be the last time we should enjoy our
comfortable little tent, for which there were
many candidates at Cairo, as none but the
most common are to be had there.

We made a considerable circuit on our
road, to what is generally believed to be the

site of Memphis. This beginning of our
ride afforded us an interesting view of
the whole range of the Pyramids. Our
Arab attendants were so little acquainted
with these localities, that it was some
time before we found the chief object
of our *détour*, the statue of Sesostris, as
it is generally called. This was also ex-
cavated by Caviglia ; it is broken off at the
ankles, and is of colossal proportions.

The pit, in which it is still recumbent,
being at this season of the year filled with
water, we could only distinguish one side of
its face, as it lies in profile, and indeed only
to the bridge of the nose, as the remainder
of that feature was quite immersed, and fortunately without mutilation, for in dry weather, the countenance, which is of a very
dignified character of expression, is said to be
seen, in perfect preservation. The arms appear broken, but not wholly detached. It is
supposed, on a little further excavation, the

feet would be found. This would prove a most valuable relic of antiquity, and be a monument more interesting, and more unique than an obelisk, particularly if placed similarly to those elevated in front of St. Peter's, and on the *Place Louis XV.*

We were followed by children, offering us medals and *real antiquities*, of which there is a regular manufactory further up the country, and so well counterfeited, that many antiquarians are believed to have been taken in. We ourselves found, what is comparatively modern, a coin of Adrian's.

The fragrance and freshness of the country was quite enchanting. Our ride was through alternate clover and bean fields, in full flower, and of a growth of which, in England, one never dreamt. We saw some barley in the ear, the fourth crop produced in this fertile soil within twelve months. Arab villages, in the middle of date forests, were dispersed among these rich and cultivated districts. Their inhabitants appeared quite a savage race ; the little children were perfectly unclothed. One would have supposed them monkeys, as they were seen climbing up the palm-trees, their skin of so dark a shade, that some of our party fancied themselves again in the West Indies, from the general effect of vegetation and climate.

A species of ibis, the stork, hawks, and every variety of aquatic bird, inhabit this bank of the Nile. From a little mountain, we imagined we were the objects of observation to some men, who stood immovable, and watched our motions with fixed attention, and the gentlemen advanced for the purpose of facing, what turned out to be large vultures. As they are superstitiously believed to anticipate their carnivorous repast, we began to ask each other, and ourselves, if we were quite well, and the wholesome effect of our late style of journeyings caused our being satisfactorily assured in the affirmative.

We passed the plain ascertained to be that on which the Israelites worked for their hard taskmasters, not only from the fact that its clay still furnishes materials for brick-work, but that lately an excavation had been made near the spot, and many thousands of skulls have been dug up from what may be supposed a burying-ground, and that the peculiar form of the skull was quite distinct from that of the Egyptian, and I believe the bone varied in colour. On being shewn the two kinds, the difference of character was certainly very strongly defined.

We had intended to visit the Polytechnic School, at Boulac, of which Mehemet Ali is said to be very justly proud, but our circuit to the pyramids had extended our ride to more than twenty miles, and neither daylight nor our tired donkeys allowed us to make any further peregrinations. It was so dark when we got back into the narrow little streets of Cairo, that we quite lost sight of each other, and our gentlemen, most ungallantly, but we believe, unconsciously, reached the hotel long before Minney and myself, and received us as *if* they had been much alarmed at having missed us.

We found our Athens acquaintance, Mr. J. de L——, who was just arrived from Thebes, with a series of beautiful daguerrotypes of all the principal monuments. He gave a very indifferent report of Lord A——'s progress, who had to contend with a lazy crew and a cowardly leader, and was laying to at Essouan, where he hoped we should overtake him. Sir Thomas and Lady M'M——n, with a very pretty daughter, were just arrived, on their way to Bombay. They gave us no fresh news, as they left London occupied alone with the Queen's approaching marriage.

JANUARY 11TH.—Our letters at last arrived, and were as satisfactory as we could desire. Happily, all my *pressentimens* of evil with regard to the children were so falsified, that I determined never again to listen to my superstitious misgivings. No tidings of our boats.

I went to a real Turkish bath, which I had secured for the one hour in which the public are excluded. I found it perfectly delightful, and much more comfortably arranged, than the private one at Nourri Effendi's harem, at Constantinople, although that was on a more luxurious scale; for here the towels were neither of pink silk, nor with silver and gold embroidery.

The heat is for some time very oppressive, but the charm of the repose succeeding is not to be described, and I very unwillingly left the couch on which I had been placed, by the summons of the *handmaid*, with a glass of sherbet, which was the signal of my having spent my permitted time at the bath.

JANUARY 12TH.—Attended Mr. Leider's

chapel. We passed through the handsomest quarter of Cairo, where it was intended to establish the hotels and the Frank residence, but Egyptian prejudices against allowing infidel dogs the best quarters Mehemet Ali found too strong to contend with.

The Princess's palace was pointed out to us as the house in which *Kleber* was assassinated, and the one opposite as the headquarters of Napoleon. The fact of the Pacha having, a few years ago, assigned it to Lord Waterford, for his residence, was mentioned as a matter of equal historical importance. A European nobleman's visit to Cairo was then a much more rare occurrence than it has lately become ; one is a little *desillusionnée* about the East, where, at one hotel, you are shewn the room occupied by Lord and Lady S——n, Lord C. H——n, the Hon. Mr. L——n, *the* Baronet and his Lady, &c., &c.; in short, one does not like being reminded

of the Ship Inn at Dover, in the city of
the Pharaohs.

JANUARY 13TH.—At last our boats are
arrived. We profited by an invitation to
dine at the harem of Shami Bey, secretary to Mehemet Ali. Our interpretess
called for us at two o'clock, imagining the
dinner was at that early hour.

We found the house even handsomer than
the last at which we had visited. Black slaves
received us as we entered the court, and
shewed us the way up a fine flight of marble
steps, where there were several groups of
female slaves, of varied hue, from the Abyssinian to the Circassian, and all appeared
employed in household arrangements, preparing coffee, drawing water, arranging
fruit, &c.

The dishes and vases commonly in use
are of such classical form, that one is always
wishing to be able to trace the impressions
of such grouping, and I did not find our

residence long enough in such scenes to become less alive to their beauties.

A very pretty little woman rose at our entrance, and welcomed us with a more shy and diffident manner than we had yet met with, and seemed always to appeal to a gay-looking *amie de la maison* for subjects of conversation. At the corner of the divan, squatted a perfect old crone, who was distinguished as the doctress &c. of the harem, and who, I thought, did not look at all benignantly at us giaours. The pretty little pale woman, whose name was Saramé, was Shami Bey's daughter-in-law, and, to a certain degree, the mistress of this very large establishment.

She wore yellow silk trousers, to which, at the ankles, were attached draperies of the same material, lined with some other colour, in this instance, light blue, which gave the effect to the extremities of what a mermaid is represented to have in lieu of feet, so that

the action of walking is constantly impeded,
and a sort of shuffling pace substituted,
which is far from dignified.   Her caftan, or
jacket, was blue cloth, embroidered with
pearls, and trimmed with sable, which, at this
season, is in general use.   She wore a tight
necklace of fine pearls, with a clasp of uncut
precious stones.

Her turban was a very slight one, of black
gauze, on one side of which she had a very
handsome diamond ornament, set in the
form of a branch and flower of a pomegranate, and above it a large diamond crescent,
composed of the finest stones I had yet seen
worn.

Saramé's clear pale complexion, with a
very mild expression of countenance, and
beautiful form, conveyed the very personifi-
cation of night.   As these fair harem pri-
soners are very fond of seeing all they can
of European novelties, we put on every
possible ornament, few as we had, and

shewed them our album, which amused them very much, at least the portraits, for the landscapes they always held upside down.

Minney asked Saramé to let her try and do her picture, and succeeded in making something of a likeness, in pencil. On this they produced some red ink, for her to add colour to the cheeks, and wanted very much to send off our interpretess for our box of colours, but we resisted parting with our *mouth-piece*.

Minney was in the act of packing up her performance, when there was a regular representation of the impossibility of such a proceeding, and the reasons given were, that should my father, husband, son, or brother, see the portrait, it would be the same as if they had seen Saramé herself, and draw down upon her her father and husband's vengeance. This was more flattering to Minney's talent than it was at all intended, but it was really amusing to see the state of excitement of the whole harem, at the prospect of such a contingency.

We went down stairs to dinner into the summer apartment, a marble hall, with a beautiful fountain surrounded by a balustrade of different coloured marbles, and a chintz divan placed against it, which in June may be a most charming *locale*, but in this the month of January it felt most unseasonable.   We all appeared to be playing *at summer*, in order that our entertainment might take place in the best apartment, of which the only furniture was a wide divan of blue silk, with pink cushions, embroidered in gold with the richness of the Duke of D——n's best full-dressed coat.

We, as guests, were not presented with the silver ewer, nor was the rose-water poured on our hands by a slave on her knee, till Saramé had first gone through the ceremony. Five of the women, I suppose of her *societé intime*, sat, or rather squatted, round the tray, which was supported by the Turkish table, or what we should describe as a stool, ornamented with mother of pearl.

The dinner was really excellent, and in only too great profusion, for we could not have had less than forty dishes, handed one at a time. To avoid tasting all, our interpretess's experience made her assure our hostess that our Hakim had forbidden us eating such and such dishes, so that we *permitted* ourselves what we liked. The soup was very good, chicken powdered so finely that it looked and was as light as a soufflet; but what we most approved was, a *plât doux* of starch, with a sort of conserve of rose-leaf sauce, and some perfectly arranged salad, in which lemon or lime juice was the substitute for vinegar, and I think would be generally preferred.

At a table, (below salt I suppose,) sat

about the same number as ourselves, who succeeded to our dishes, but no one at that table took the precedence as Saramé did at ours, in presenting a pinch of each plat with her very clean and very pretty rose-tipped little fingers.

I could not help being struck with the melancholy expression of her countenance, and I supposed the visible increase of this expression was the consequence of fatigue attending her first *foreign* dinner, but it was accounted for by bad health and the loss of her two children; and that consequently her husband, thinking his first choice an unlucky one, had lately purchased a Greek slave, a pretty girl, but much less so than his present wife, and that in the event of this slave becoming mother to a son, her position in the family would be advanced.

However occasionally *distraite* poor little Saramé was with the novelty of our visit, yet her attention was constantly attracted

back to her rival, who, while waiting upon
her, evinced the most decided expression of
assumption of manner, at least so I imagined.
The ungrateful object of these heartburnings
was, at Alexandria, attached to Mehemet
Ali's court, and Saramé is said to be incon-
solable at this division of his affections,
for it seems a plurality of wives is much
less frequent, in Turkish *ménages*, than we
Europeans imagined. The climate of Egypt
is almost invariably fatal to Turkish children, and, indeed, the general mortality is
enormous.

But to return to our fête, there was only
one large candle on our dining table, en-
sconced in an embossed piece of silver,
hardly to be called a candlestick. The
lighting this large room was effected in the
prettiest way possible by the slaves, who
collected in groups, each holding a thick
candle, like those used in a Catholic
chapel.

The shadows thrown from and by these animated candlesticks, will quite spoil my taste for those of crystal and ormolu. As the bearers of these lights became tired, and occasionally supported themselves against a column or a balustrade, they would have afforded models to supersede those of the most approved modern workmanship.

On a signal given by Saramé, the living candlesticks proceeded to what I suppose may be considered the drawing-room, where the *private band* of the harem was collected, who produced their usual discordant sounds in singing accompaniments to the different dances executed by the Turkish, Arab, and Greek slaves of the harem. The strained postures of the Arab dancing was almost painful to see, but reminded us much of the cachucha, by the attitude in which the dancer throws herself backward, so that the back of the head nearly touched the ground, from the extreme elasticity of limb and body. The Greek dance was in quick time, and might have passed for an Irish jig, becoming more and more rapid. The two little dancers, who appeared to be about twelve years old, became quite exhausted with their exertions.

The chief musician, a lively-looking girl, *improvisé'd* evidently a very amusing song, as they all laughed immoderately. The fair Saramé's throwing her slipper at her proved the signal for a general romp, when they all chased one another round the room. We were then begged to dance and sing. Minney and the youngest Miss G—— organized a quadrille, in which two of the Eastern ladies were enlisted, and shewed great aptitude in both the figures and their *chassés*.

Their second-hand imitations of French dancing was very amusing, from the perfect contrast of costume and their general *desinvoltura*. Our music afterwards consisted of a chorus of " God save the King," and we were none of us sufficiently modernized to get beyond " King George our gracious King ;" and after a prolonged visit of six hours, thought it time to take leave. Pretty little Saramé had taken such a fancy to Minney, she would not let her go, and entreated me to leave her, I suppose as *dame de compagnie.*

The court was quite lighted by torches carried by our donkey attendants, and those borne by the black slaves of the harem, whom we found following us home for *backshish.* Our whole visit seemed to realize the description of a sultana's feast in the Arabian Nights. The confinement of even this, their best existence, makes one feel a degree of compassion for them, which I am told and hope is quite misapplied.

CHAPTER XII.

Boulac—Joseph's well—Stores of grain—A rhino-
ceros—Embark on board a Nile boat—Discomforts
of the voyage—A strange meeting—Arrival at the
gates of Alexandria—Difficulties in getting admitted—Mehemet Ali—His palace.

JANUARY 14TH.—We went to Boulac to
visit our boats, which we found tolerably
good, and well calculated for the longer
voyage we had projected. We next visited
Joseph's well, and found we had mistaken
the spot where the sycamore tree stands,
described as the one under which the Virgin
reposed in their flight to Egypt. It is said

to have the property of being always green,
and this is ascribed to its sacred character.
It may stand near the original spot, but
naturalists assert that this tree itself is only
of the growth of six centuries. We found
that the ruins, said to be the remains of the
prison of the patriarch Joseph, are shewn at
Heliopolis.

The site of the old palace of the Pharaohs
is sufficiently defined, (or believed to be so,)
by antiquaries, to give a shadow of probability that the ruins of the contiguous prison
may be still visible.

We were much struck by the piles of corn
and beans in the environs of Boulac. One
felt that Joseph's preparations for the years
of famine must have resembled these mounds
of plenty. The summits were to be distinguished at a great height above the very
high walls of the courts in which they were
preserved, and in front of the Polytechnic
school there was a *mountain* of barley, which

must have far surpassed in height the mound formerly at the entrance into Kensington gardens. No wonder that the coats of the mules and donkeys are so sleek, with such abundant and good provender.

Our boatmen assure us they shall be ready *boukra* (to-morrow), but as that is the constant answer of an Arab to all inquiries or reproaches, one hardly can trust to this habitual and procrastinating reply.

JANUARY 15TH.—We called to make some farewell visits, and found that in this instance yesterday's *boukra* became to-day, and that our Arabs were anxious to leave after sunset, their favourite hour for starting on a voyage. The noise, wind, and dust, of this most picturesque of cities, made us leave it without regret. We settled ourselves very comfortably in our boats, but from the difficulty of dividing our numbers, we were obliged to make one boat the harem; and by this arrangement we could only meet at dinner, when the boats must be stopped, and tied together. We felt that our month's voyage to Thebes would have proved somewhat unsociable, and in spite of all the *agrémens* of our journeyings, we all rejoiced that we were making the first steps to our several father-lands.

JANUARY 16TH.—The day cold, and occasionally rainy, the wind strong, and against us, with much motion of the boat, varied by our constantly getting aground. We were all thoroughly uncomfortable, and even *indisposed*, which I have thought impossible, in river navigation.

The Arabs were more obstinate and lazy than those of the Desert. A constant wrangling was going forward, to make the boatmen row, as the sail was worse than useless. The wind fell after sunset, and we were all a little comforted by our re-union at dinner: our sociable enjoyment was soon disturbed, by an invitation to separate after coffee, that we might endeavour to recover our lost day ; our advance, in spite of having had a double set of rowers, to relieve each other, having been only twenty miles in more than that number of hours.

The night was so cold, we could hardly get to sleep, but the consequent absence of buzzing and biting creatures consoled me for everything, and we did not see any of the rats we heard of as dreadful monopolizers of the lower part of the boat, although they had nearly devoured our books, dates, and figs.

JANUARY 17TH.—We passed rather a quieter day, and were assured the progress we had made would enable us to reach the canal of Mahmoudie the next day.

Just as it was becoming dusk, we, according to the approved Nile fashion, (from Thebes to Alexandria,) hailed a boat we met, and inquired where they were going, and who was on board. The inquiry was answered by a lady with a very Scotch accent, who informed us she was going up to the Cataracts, and had been very lately under water, as the lazy crew of her boat had crowded so much sail, that it had been upset. She appeared to have no European companions, and I believe one would not find a lady of any other nation with so great a spirit of independence.

JANUARY 18TH.—Reached Adfé about eight o'clock, A.M., but the announced track-boat had not arrived. We were obliged to have recourse to a light boat, which could, with difficulty, contain four people, so that we left the doctor and the remainder of the party, to follow us, in the slower and heavier boat. We had the greatest difficulty in getting on, as the violent rain not only greatly incommoded us, but made the path-side of the canal so slippery, that the single horse towing our boat could hardly make his way.

At the third relay we were troubled with a very vicious beast, who kicked, plunged, and occasionally ran away, which gave so much motion to our little vessel, (not larger than a gondola,) that we suffered some hair-breadth escapes of being capsized. We contrived to dine, thanks to some cold chickens we had seized in the hurry of departure, and very fortunately, as we were twelve hours making a journey of forty miles, of which eight hours is the average time.

At last we reached a wharf near Alexandria, thoroughly worn out, and partially wet through, for we could not close the front door of our cabin without risk of suffocation. George proceeded to the gate of Alexandria, nearly two miles off, leaving us under the care of the reiz of our boat, a civil man, but with whom we could not exchange a word. Owing to the said reiz not having obtained the pass-word at the last village where we changed horse, George could not gain admittance at the gate of the city.

The custode either did not, or would not, understand his request to send up some message to our consul to obtain our *sesame*. He returned to us in great tribulation, and we were perfectly at a loss where and how we could possibly pass this rainy night. Our reiz contrived to make us understand his suggestions of offering to appeal to the guardian of the Viceroy's track-boat, to give us permission to pass the night under its shelter. This request was hospitably granted, and we made our establishment in the saloon, where the ottoman afforded us dry, though narrow bedding, and we had nothing to complain of but absence of food, as none could be procured outside the gates at this late hour.

The Arab had a little fire, which afforded us hot water, to which the addition of a little Eau-de-Cologne, proved very satisfactory. This I mention as a hint to any travellers who may find themselves in an equally benighted condition. It was very odd that, at the approach of nearly the most civilized point of our journey, we should have met with the greatest degree of inconvenience.

JANUARY 19TH.—Our arrival having been early reported, Mr. Waghorn sent some of the valuable donkey race to take us into Alexandria. We were quite surprised at the cheerful and European aspect of the town, and were soon comfortably lodged in an excellent French hotel, superior to any at Marseilles, although the *Aubergistes*, and nearly everything else, are imported from that city.

We held *salon* all day, so numerous were our visitors among the Consular authorities. The kind attentions of Ex-Consul-General Campbell and regnant Colonel Hodges, made up a good deal for our numerous *contretems* at Cairo, in the letter and boat line. Doctor

Moore, of New York, professor of Greek Literature, an old acquaintance of George's, joined us at dinner, and gave us an account of the *almost* revolution that had lately taken place at Athens, from whence he was just arrived.

There was much excitement at Alexandria, owing to the report of a meditated attack on Mehemet Ali, to oblige him to restore the Turkish fleet. Many Europeans had packed up their goods, to be prepared against a speedy removal, but Mehemet Ali's assurance that all European property should be respected, had already greatly allayed the panic occasioned by this rumour of war.

JANUARY 20TH.—Mons. Tibaldi came for us in Seyd Bey's boat, that we might obtain a good view of the Pacha, who, according to his daily habit, was to inspect one of the Turkish ships, and without previous notice as to the one he should select for that purpose. He always goes on board alone, and unarmed, descending into the hold, and entering into every minutiæ with regard to the service of the ship. That he should thus venture into the *enemy's camp*, without any precaution, is consistent with all his former conduct, and with the spirit of fatalism, which pervades all his actions.

On one occasion he was complimented for his activity in getting on board, and for not being disturbed by a rough gale. This he accounted for very simply by saying, that in early life he had been pressed as a sailor, and served for a considerable time on board a small brig. Subsequently, it seems, he was waiter at a coffee-house at —— in Roumelia.

After remaining for some time in vain expectation of his appearance, we determined upon going to the arsenal, where Mons. Tibaldi suspected the pacha might have remained, to assist at the launch of an iron steamer. There we succeeded in meeting him, and we had, under Monsieur T.'s escort, an opportunity of being quite close to the Viceroy, and presented, as far as ladies could be. I never saw so striking and intelligent a countenance, or one with half the variety of expression, the eye had at one moment that of positive benevolence, and an instant afterwards, when some of the machinery went wrong, it gained the most savage expression ; and again, when an awkward-looking boy fell down in turning a wheel, it assumed an appearance of fun and mischief, accompanied by a chuckle, for one could hardly call it a laugh.

His costume was very simple—a greenish brown suit, trimmed with ugly light fur, and a red fez, (cap,) and he wore pea-green silk gloves ! His cloak was held up by one attendant, more as if for the purpose of keeping it out of the dirt than for ceremony. The Capitan Pacha was on his left, and Burghos Bey, his prime minister, and five or six others, stood near him, but there was no appearance

Drawn on stone by R. J. Hamerton   drawn from the original by ___

M E H E M E T

Published by Henry Colburn, 13 Great Marlborough Street, 1836

of the etiquette of a court. The only
smart thing belonging to him was his large
cherry-coloured parasol, trimmed with gold
fringe, of which an ill-dressed Arab was in
charge, but which the heat of the day did
not oblige him to unfurl.

We were told that, except Mrs. Light,
who went in male costume to his levee, no
European ladies had ever been in such direct
communication with him. One of our party
who had been residing at Alexandria for
eight years, had never before seen him but at
a great distance. He seemed to be very much
amused as well as flattered at our anxiety
to see him, and remarked that Minney
must be the youngest European lady traveller
of her time. All this was communicated
through the medium of his interpreter in
Turkish. He professes to know no other
language, but I thought, as our answers in
French were translated, he frequently appeared to have forestalled the interpreter.

We then went to see his palace, which is furnished in modern and indifferent French taste. His room of reception was floored with English oilcloth; I think his divan was also covered with English chintz. The room contained no other furniture, unless some very large glazed mahogany cases of stuffed birds, and some ill-painted sea-pieces could come under that head. We returned by the back of the palace, to avoid meeting the Pacha, on his return by water from the arsenal, and thus exposing him to too much of our society; but we signally failed in this, our modest attempt, as his caprice brought him back on horseback, by the very road we had chosen. He rode a very pretty bay horse, richly caparisoned, and appeared to much advantage, as it gave him the effect of greater height than he naturally possesses.

We heard an amusing instance of his pretended naïveté, which occurred a few days ago, as he discussed the question of the combination formed by the allied powers to oblige him to give up the fleet. When Prussia was named, he asked in what quarter of the world it was situated, as he said he was made fully aware of the existence of Russians, French, Austrians, Dutch, and English, by their shipping and their commercial relations, but he had inquired, and never could hear of a Prussian ship having been in any of his ports.

He did not begin to learn to read till after fifty, and his reasons for then doing so are rather curious. It seems that illiterate Turks are subject to constant interruption on their time; and Mehemet Ali found this so inconvenient, that he adopted what is always considered a protection—holding a book; in short, appearing occupied in study; and he found, after some time, that it would be agreeable really to do what he only pretended: so began his *a b c* in good earnest.

He is not, however, supposed to be able to write, beyond giving his official signature.

He has lately, under pretence of affording instruction to the Turkish fleet, decimated Egyptian officers and men in all their ships. This assumption of the superiority of the Egyptian navy is perfectly justified by appearances.

Under the excuse of refitting the Turkish sailors, he has clothed several hundreds in his uniforms, of which he announced he had a large provision for which he had no actual use. It is, however, whispered, that within a short period the Egyptian tailors had been hard at their needles, by the Pacha's orders; and this is the result.

CHAPTER XIII.

Pompey's pillar—The Pacha and the Sultan's portrait
—A ball at Alexandria—Seyd Bey's palace—Sin-
gular bequest—Sir M. M...... and the Pacha—
The garden of the palace—The fleet at Alexandria
—Preparations for departure, and reflections on re-
turning to England.

JANUARY 21ST.—Mr. Joyce, one of the
principal merchants in Egypt, drove us to
see Pompey's pillar, which, notwithstanding
it is said to be so inferior in height and
proportions to our Monument, or the Co-
lonne de la Place Vendôme, is much more
striking than either, as you stand immediately under it ; but this may be owing to

its more isolated and elevated position. How people have managed to reach its summit by kites and rope-ladders, (and one of these, Baroness Talbot,) it is impossible to imagine, for there does not appear to be the smallest support afforded by inequality of surface ; the pedestal and shaft being each of a single block of granite, and measuring upwards of a hundred feet in height. Cleopatra's needle we satisfied ourselves with seeing from Mr. Larking's balcony, and from thence his good glass enabled us to distinguish the point of Aboukeir.

JANUARY 22ND.—No sight-seeing—the weather rainy. The incident of the day, however, was the request of the Pacha to see our album. On looking it over he observed that the young Sultan's picture could not be a correct likeness, as it represented a young man with a beard, and that Abdul Megid being a boy of only sixteen, could not have that manly ornament ; Mons. Chacaton, however, modestly insisted on the portrait being faithful in that respect; so, to decide the matter, his highness sent for the Capitan Pacha, (the late Turkish traitor,) who confirmed Monsieur C.'s assertion. This was followed by the request, that we would give the Pacha a copy of the picture of his Sovereign and Master. It was rather suspected that this conversation was got up for the purpose of speaking of himself as vassal to the young Sultan. A large dinner party at Mr. Joyce's, of all the authorities of Alexandria. Mrs. Joyce had given herself the trouble of arranging a little dance in the evening for the amusement of Minney, who was much charmed with her African *début* in society. There were at least one hundred and sixty members of the Alexandrian *world* —many of the Levantines very pretty, but they had dressed in the worst European taste, instead of profiting by their own pretty costume. The band was black, and the floor stone.

JANUARY 23RD.—We drove to see Seyd
Bey's palace and pretty garden.   The rooms
were of beautiful proportions, and the furniture in European, and in rather Louis
XIV. taste, though somewhat scantily dispersed.

Seyd is distinguished as the Pacha's
favourite son—one would imagine on the
principle of contrast, for no one can look
less intellectual. Although only eighteen,
he is an old and larger likeness of Mr. S.
M—y, thinking of nothing but what and
how much he should eat, and taking every
opportunity of giving foreigners breakfasts
and dinners on board his frigate.   The
pacha encourages this for the sake of exercising him in European languages.   He
speaks French very fluently, and, besides
following up the branches of his naval profession, he is crammed with mathematics and
political economy, and is treated exactly
like a schoolboy.

He was not allowed to *assist* at Mrs. Joyce's ball, because he had that day neglected his English lesson, and the Pacha threatens him with dismissal from all favours, if he cannot speak English perfectly in six months. As with Mehemet Ali will is law, I dare say he will soon have acquired the language, even to a cockney accent.

George had a long and interesting audience with the Pacha, who generally contrives to prolong an interview when he meets with a communicative European. George was particularly struck by the high-bred manner and benignity of his address. In looks he reminded him of the late Mr. S. W——. He questioned George very closely about his Syrian travels, and evaded very ingeniously his remark upon the unexpected and unaccountable quarantine at Al Arish. Mons. Tibaldi had afterwards to answer a great many inquiries as to George's politics and position in society, and also with regard to my family and connexions. On such subjects his general curiosity is quite unaccountable.

On his affording him such an opening, Mons. T. mentioned my wish of having a lock of his hair, to add to a collection, I had been for some years making, of the hair of celebrated personages. This was a request very difficult to elude, but he contrived, with his usual ingenuity, to get over my *infidel* request.

He said, that in a collection which contained Nelson's, Napoleon's, and Wellington's hair, his was as yet unworthy to be included ; but if posterity judged otherwise, he would leave in his will a request to Ibrahim Pacha to present me with his beard, and if I did not outlive him, it was to descend to my son, or the daughter who inherited my collection. The ages and names of my children were asked for, and these testamentary arrangements were very gravely made, and written down by the secretary sent for for that purpose.

In the evening, at a little party at Capt. L.'s, we heard all Alexandria was ringing with this little episode. We were at first amused at finding all resident Europeans in Egypt talking and thinking of the Pacha, as if he were the only interesting living character; but there is something so striking and original in all this old man says and does, that I am sure a prolonged residence in the Egyptian world would bring us all to the same conviction.

JANUARY 24TH.—Delay of a day in consequence of our government steam-boat, the *Blazer*, requiring some repair to her wheel, and it being the Mahometan sabbath, no work could be done at the dock-yard till after sun-set. The Jewish and Mahometan sabbaths following each other, produced rather an amusing occurrence attending Sir M. M——'s late visit to Alexandria, when he was much confined to time, as I believe the steamer that was conveying him to

Syria could only remain forty-eight hours at Alexandria, where he much wished to have an interview with the Pacha on matters of great commercial importance.

He landed late on Thursday night, and sent immediately to ask for an audience on the following day, which the Pacha declined, on the score that it would interrupt his religious duties, but appointed the day after, which equally interfered with those of Sir M. M——. In consequence of the badness of the weather, and the distance of more than two miles to the Viceroy's palace, Sir M. M—— was unable to walk, and as his religious scruples prevented him from using any beast of burthen, he had at last recourse to a sort of sedan chair, for which he, with difficulty, procured bearers.

He set off in full-dress costume, with his massive sheriff's chain, and a military hat and feather. This unusual appearance naturally created a good deal of observation, and one of the Pacha's inferior attendants announced that he had seen a dressed image in a glass box, carried into the palace, sent from the English idolaters.

We took a walk in the garden of the palace, which is pretty from looking immediately on the sea. Adjoining it, is what was the Pacha's harem, but is now converted into a lodging for *illustrious strangers*. The only remains of the live stock of the harem are said to be two of his wives, of very respectable and advanced ages ; one of whom, from her literary attainments, affords him the pleasure of reading to him the translations of the most interesting articles in the English and French papers. This recreation he only allows himself after nine in the evening, when all his official labours are ended for the day.

We dined at our Vice-Consul's, very agreeably, and accompanied Mrs. Larking to a pretty but very hot little theatre, where we were joined by Monsieur and Madame Barot, brother of Odillon, the deputy. They were just married, and going into perfect exile, by Mons. Barot's accepting the situation of Consul at Manilla. I thought her a very pretty and enterprising young French-woman ; but she proved to be one of our own countrywomen, a daughter of the scientific Captain Manby.

We called to take leave of Mons. and Madame Pastrée, from whom we had met with great attention and civility. We regretted much having missed Mons. and Madame Joseph Pastrée, another branch of the family, who had gone up the Nile. Mons. Chacaton went to the Pacha's levée, for the purpose of giving the last touches to Mehemet Ali's portrait, which is generally considered the best likeness ever done of him. Our Consul was unable to give us a clean bill of health, which was the more provoking, as, had we sailed on the day originally fixed, the suspicious cases of plague would not then have been officially reported. The circumstance of Doctor Bendiner separating from us, to shorten his voyage, by returning through Trieste, caused general regret. Although his talents had had little occasion to be exercised in our own cause, we congratulated ourselves on the reflection that he was of eminent service to the numerous sick poor we everywhere found on our path; his care, trouble, and kindness, were directed with much talent, and were bestowed with real good-will, and we feel it will be always a source of satisfaction to him as well as to ourselves to look back on the circumstances which attended his accompanying us to the East.

JAN. 25.—Owing to our Ex-Consul-General Campbell's departure on board the *Blazer*, our last African drive was in a procession consisting of all the respectable Alexandrian authorities, who accompanied him on board.

The day was bright and beautiful, and the general effect of the magnificently-manned fleet of about sixty men-of-war was heightened by the view of the Pacha and the accompanying boats, full of his attendants, rowing through it close to our steamer. The appearance was that of a splendid regatta; and, that nothing should be wanting to brighten the scene, a beautiful double rainbow served as a *cadre* to the more distant shipping.

The happy feeling that we were making our way towards home, made us so excited and joyous, that it caused the whole party to be unusually inattentive to the call of dinner, which was heard as we were losing sight of the port and its animated beauties.

The whole night fine, and my comfort on board very materially increased, by our obliging Commander, Mr. Waugh, giving me up his comfortable cabin, making me inde-

pendent of the ladies' apartment, where there were several Indian lady passengers, who were hardly yet able to bear light or air.

CHAPTER XIV.

Effects of a double rainbow—Security from lightning
in a steam-boat—Unfavourable weather—Fearful
storms — Its effects on the passengers — Alarm
—Weather improves—A general thanksgiving—
Arrival at Malta—In quarantine.

JANUARY 26TH.—The weather fine, at
least without rain, but the wind so high, it
was with difficulty we ladies could keep our
footing; but by choosing the lowest and
most sheltered positions, we contrived to
remain on deck the greatest part of the
afternoon.

In conversing with some of the officers,

we happened to advert to the fineness of the preceding day, and the beauty of the effect of what had appeared to us, a double rainbow; on which one of the older sailors shook his head very significantly, and remarked that

> " A rainbow in morning
> Is sailors' sad warning,"

and that the wind had already shifted to a foul quarter. Our advance was consequently much impeded, and our expectations of arriving at Malta on the fifth day were considerably lessened.

JANUARY 27TH.—The day cloudy, but to escape the closeness of our parlour cabin, where the windows were constantly shut by chilly and invalid passengers, we remained on deck, and listened to a discussion with regard to steam being a non-conductor of electricity; one passenger asserting, that on this account a steam-boat had the advantage of being secure against lightning. All this was delivered in very scientific language, when, our Commander coming up and hearing the subject of conversation, said he regretted very much to destroy so comfortable a theory, as the *Blazer*, the very ship we were now on board of, had been considerably damaged by lightning on a voyage from Beyrout the July before. However, we consoled ourselves with the idea, that it was improbable that the only steam-boat that had ever been struck by lightning should again suffer from the same cause ; and likewise, that we were now sailing at the very opposite season to that in which the accident had occurred.

On going below, we found the table corded round, to serve as a *point d'appui* to our plates and glasses, so much had the motion of the ship increased. It blew what the officers called *fresh*, but what appeared to me to deserve a stronger term, as one could not remain steady without clinging for support to the cots, or holding the sides of the vessel.

JANUARY 28TH.—The swell increasing, and the wind being contrary, we had not made more than forty-eight knots during twenty-four hours. The increase of motion had rendered it necessary to secure even the dining-room chairs by cords; they, however, were little occupied, as general *malaise* prevailed among the passengers, and only the persevering whist party stood their ground till ten, when we all retired to our berths, but not to rest, as the wind blew in violent and fearful gusts, which made the motion of the steamer quite intolerable, as each heavy wave struck the bottom of our little vessel.

The Commander came down, saying the night was pitch dark and rainy, with symptoms of a regular gale of wind. This prediction was very speedily verified. A violent shower of hail was the precursor, followed by loud peals of thunder, with vivid flashes of forked lightning, which played up and down the iron rigging with fearful rapidity. At one moment the flash passed so immediately between the Commander and the man at the wheel, that each believed the other struck by it. The sea, which had been getting up during the last forty-eight hours, now rose mountains high, and lashed the sides of the ship with such fury, that there were moments when those on deck thought she would not live through the trial.

She presently was struck by a sea, which came over the paddle boxes, soon followed by another, which, coming over the forecastle, effected an entrance through the skylights and left four feet of water in the officers' cabin. The vessel seemed disabled by this stunning blow; the bowsprit and fore part of the ship were for some moments under water, and the officer stationed at that part of the ship described her as appearing, during that time, to be evidently sinking; and declared that for many seconds he saw only sea. The natural buoyancy of the ship at last allowed her to right herself, and during the short lull (of three minutes) her head was turned, to avoid the danger of running too near the coast of Lybia, which, to the more experienced, was the principal cause of alarm; for had the wheels given way, which was not improbable, from the strain they had undergone, nothing could have saved us, though we had been spared all other causes for apprehension.

From my little cabin, which was immediately at the foot of the stairs, and where I had been joined by George, we distinctly heard all that passed on deck.

" She will never make head against such another sea."

" I never witnessed such a gale."

" The lightning has struck the ship!"

" Batten down the hatches !"

" What can be done for those poor women below ?" &c.

These remarks made our Commander's more reassuring language very little effective, as he repeatedly came down to inquire after us. The cries of poor Mrs. S—— to her husband, not to leave her, as she gave herself up to despair, were the only sounds of distress we heard. Mrs. S. P——, (another Indian passenger, who was taking her little girl to England,) remained perfectly still, though nearly dead from terror. Poor Christine was very composed, but touched me much by the proof she afforded of unselfishness at the moment of danger.

    *   *   *   *   *   *   *

    *   *   *   *   *   *   *

Minney did not wake till the dreadful rush of water into the cabin.

    *   *   *   *   *   *   *

    *   *   *   *   *   *   *

The only passenger who left his side of the ship for ours, was Mr. C . . . r, who, during the early part of the evening, had been talking to me of his prospects of happiness, in so soon rejoining his wife and children, from whom he had been separated for some years, by a prolonged residence in India. He had gone on deck at the moment the storm seemed at its height, and on coming down to us, suggested that we should not satisfy ourselves by praying privately for deliverance from such imminent peril, but begged that he might join in our supplications, and in humbling ourselves before Heaven, from whence alone we could expect help.

I succeeded in reaching the fore-cabin, which I at first thought impracticable, as even the steward could not keep his footing. Poor Mrs. S——'s appearance first struck me ; she appeared like a beautiful spectre, pale as ashes, with her long black hair falling over her shoulders. On communicating to her and Mrs. P——, Mr. C...r's proposition of our assembling to join in prayer, it was met with the greatest eagerness and gratitude.

We all knelt round the cabin, as Mr. C...r made a very simple but forcible prayer. A moment of calm seemed restored to the minds of the most agitated, during this act of short, but I believe most intense devotion.

I never can forget the moments of agony I passed previously to this period, deeply touched by the calmness of ——— who appeared to be only conscious of the degree of danger to which Minney and myself were exposed.

* * * * * * *

* * * * * * *

For although there was not a moment in which I lost all hope, yet the image of death was most strongly before me, and I trust I shall never cease to remember the train of awful reflections it suggested, and the feelings of gratitude towards Heaven with which I was impressed, and which various circumstances so powerfully excited during our time of peril.

* * * * * * *

* * * * * * *

* * * * * * *

With daylight the fearful part of the hurricane gave way, and we were now in the direction of Candia, no longer indeed contending against the wind, but the sea still surging and impetuous, and no lull taking place during twelve hours, to afford the opportunity of regaining our track, from which we had deviated about 150 miles. The sea had so completely deluged the lower part of the ship, that it was with difficulty that sufficient fire could be made to afford us even coffee for breakfast. Dinner was not to be thought of.

I was persuaded to go on deck, to see

what was called *a fine sight*, but the still
tremendous height of the waves caused my
feelings to be much more akin to terror
than admiration, and the idea I heard suggested, that the wind bespoke a fresh gale,
was not encouraging.

All on deck seemed to agree in the impression of our last night's peril, and one
of the officers, who had been in the navy
thirty years, confessed that, even in the
West Indies, he had never witnessed a worse
storm, or felt in greater jeopardy. At nightfall the ship was turned from the direction
of Candia, and although the sea was still
very rough, from not yet having had time to
subside, we had reason to be satisfied that
all was *again right*.

I found myself much more unreasonably
nervous and incessant in my inquiries after
the weather, than in the moment of real
cause for alarm. I was absurdly annoyed
by a beautiful Newfoundland dog belonging
to the ship taking refuge in my cabin, as he

had done the preceding night, which circumstance had then been superstitiously
remarked upon by his *ship-mates* as quite an
unusual proceeding. The fact of seeing our
Commander fast asleep, was much more reassuring to me than any other argument against
my fears, as I felt convinced he would not
be absent from the deck were his presence
the least necessary.

JANUARY 30TH.—The weather beautiful.
I found it almost impossible to believe it the
same sea, it now wore such a calm and placid
smile. All our passengers assembled in the
ladies' cabin, that Mrs. S—— and Mrs.
P——, who were not able to leave it, might
join in the heartfelt thanksgiving which Mr.
C . . . r read us, from the beautiful form of
service in our church liturgy.

In the evening the doctor reported un-
favourably with respect to Mr. J——, the
late chief-justice of Ceylon, and a poor East
Indian servant of General S——'s, who, from
his berth having been completely under water

the preceding night, had caught cold, and was now in a violent state of delirious fever.

JANUARY 31ST.—The fine weather continued, and we made five knots an hour, notwithstanding the damage occasioned by the loss of two paddles to each of our wheels. We remained on deck during the whole of this beautiful evening.

FEBRUARY 1ST.—The day most enjoyable. We saw Mount Etna distinctly, though at the distance of 110 miles; sailed by the light-house of the harbour of Malta just at sunset, and therefore too late to be admitted into the lazaretto, but we were promised this day should count. Our bill of health, though marked only as suspicious, condemned us to the extended quarantine attending a foul one; but to arrive, and hear such fresh news of Europe, was quite happiness enough to make us overlook any other consideration.

FEBRUARY 2ND.—We found Sir Henry Bouverie had secured for us the most comfortable quarters, at Fort Manuel, opposite those prepared for Sir Robert Stopford, on his return from Vourla. We collected furniture to add to our own provision, and soon found ourselves most comfortably established; our view of the sea and the harbour very pretty, and nothing served to remind us of being in quarantine, but the fear the guardians shewed of our touching them, a lady having lately caused the Capitano to be detained in the Lazaretto for fourteen days, by having touched him with her parasol! The melancholy death of the poor Indian servant, which occurred two days after our arrival, gave us some cause to apprehend that our twenty-one days' quarantine would be reckoned from the day of the poor man's burial.

END OF THE DIARY.

APPENDIX.

(No. I.)

THOUGHTS ON THE QUESTION OF THE EAST.

BY THE HON. COLONEL DAMER.

THE writer of these pages having lately passed some months in the Levant, where he had opportunities of judging those countries with his own eyes, and likewise the advantage of hearing from well-informed persons the views of all parties concerned, directly or indirectly, in the momentous question that now agitates Europe; having also given that question much anxious consideration; he cannot bring his mind to any other conclusion than that England appears to be acting not only in great ignorance of the real state of affairs in the East of Europe, but is manifestly losing sight of what is also to her a matter of high import, how that question is connected with her interests in India.

It has been, he believes, assumed (an assumption founded on the personal dislike the late Sultan Mahmoud was known to bear Mehemet Ali,) that the latter is in reality, though secretly, the friend of Russia; it is possible that this sentiment may have been in some degree imbibed by our Ambassador at the Porte, and that his enthusiastic but honest zeal for the Turkish empire may in consequence have led him to look upon every act or proposition of the Pacha pretty much as the late Sultan himself would do were he alive.

The writer has reason to think it true, that six months ago, when the allied powers announced to the world their determination to settle the affairs of the East, the Porte

was then on the point of sending a nego-
tiator to Mehemet Ali with such powers,
and with such instructions, as would in
all probability have insured the tranquil
arrangement of the dispute without the
interference of any third party ; and it is
also well known that the Sultan had already
made in January, 1837, through the medium
of Sarem Effendi (who was afterwards for a
short time Reis Effendi), much more favourable proposals to the Pacha than those
offered to him now, viz., the sovereignty of
Egypt, with two out of the four pachalics
of Syria, which would have given to him
Damascus, the seaport of Beyrout, and the
fortress of St. Jean d'Acre.

It seems that little is known of the Pacha's
character and disposition, and still less is
remembered of his services to the Porte
during a long career. He it was who
fought the battles of the Turks in Greece ;
and if the game was there lost, and the

Morea finally subdued, the Turks have to accuse their own want of energy and fore-thought, and not to blame the lack of skill in the Pacha, who foresaw and warned the Sultan that if he did not make more haste, and display more vigour, the classical interest that had been excited in Europe in favour of Greece, would lead to active measures being adopted for its liberation, and he foretold that possession of that country would be finally snatched from his grasp.

On looking into this question, one cannot fail to perceive, that it is very much the classical enthusiasm in favour of Greece, by which England, in common with other nations, allowed itself to be carried away, that has led to the lamentable state in which that kingdom, once an important portion of the Ottoman dominions, is now plunged, and which has brought us by rapid strides to the present crisis, where we witness on the one hand the Ottoman empire, dispossessed of Greece, the Morea, and the principal Greek islands, quickly approaching its end, and Russia eager and ready to seize upon her prey. On the other, we see a sturdy vassal, with powers of mind and firmness of no ordinary stamp, strengthened by conquest, elated and encouraged by success, who has established for himself a position of real power which it is idle to deny and not easy to contend with.

It is believed to be a fact, that Mehemet Ali has no wish to throw off his subjection to the Porte; he is not and never was the ally of Russia, and if, from the number of Frenchmen employed in his service, he has appeared to be under the influence of France, such impressions have been raised on incorrect premises; for but a slight knowledge of the man would suffice to give conviction, that no one is so well aware of what are his real interests as himself, and that his decided tendencies are to an English alliance.

It is right to add here, that the number of French in his employ has much diminished of late, and that if he has had so many of them, it has been because we threw him into the arms of the French, our government having refused his application that British officers should be allowed to enter his service, and all Englishmen in general having been discouraged from attaching themselves to him. The French, as a nation, have little influence with him.

The principal merchants in Egypt and Syria are, with one exception, British. There is but one considerable French house at Alexandria; and the preference of us by his son, Ibrahim Pacha, is said to be so decided, that he has but one officer in his service of French descent, and he is a gentleman of Levantine birth and education.

Whereas, in other respects, he is either served by English, or by Egyptians, whom he had sent to England to be educated.

It is just now undoubtedly to be apprehended, that the friendship and protection of France shewn to the Pacha at such an important crisis of his affairs, when all the other great powers seem to be arrayed against him, cannot fail to have its effects on him. But matters having reached this height is but a natural consequence of the false direction given to our diplomacy in the East; and they will, without doubt, right themselves, when England and the Pacha shall better comprehend their true positions, and recur to those principles of self-interest and mutual defence which ought, and will, sooner or later, promote and establish an alliance that will prove equally beneficial and desirable to both.

The writer of these pages is convinced that Mehemet Ali has every wish to remain a vassal of the Porte; that is to say, a useful, serviceable vassal; but the Porte has conceived and encouraged a violent hatred to the man, and has too often affected to despise and underrate his power. What have been the consequences? Two successful campaigns, in which the Turkish armies, if not annihilated, were so defeated, so disorganized, and dispersed, that Russia alone prevented the onward march of the victorious army, and its occupation of Constantinople; on one occasion, I may remark, when our fleet was cruizing in the North Sea, watching the Dutch!

Is then Mehemet Ali not a conqueror? has he not a fair right to terms in some degree adequate to his former services? If this be not conceded, has he not claims, after having captured the whole of the Turkish artillery, wasted and destroyed all means of annoyance the Porte single-handed could bring against him, and having only stopped the progress of his troops when they were on the eve of knocking at the door of the capital itself; has he not claims, it may be asked, to a fair consideration of his demands in the present posture of affairs in the East?

It may here be well to call attention to the circumstance, that it was Mehemet Ali who conquered the Whahabees, and preserved for the Porte possession of Arabia; without his aid the Porte would have lost that country. He now keeps up there an army of 40,000 men, and defends, for the Porte, the Holy Cities, which he alone is able to do, and without which possession, all *prestige*—all those illusions and traditions which hold the Mussulman empire together, and form the sacred and religious links by which it is bound, would at once be loosened and finally dissolved.

Mehemet Ali wishes to remain powerful and wealthy; he has some claims to so

much ambition.   He is anxious to remain
the vassal of the Porte, and is indeed persuaded (and late events would seem to
justify the pretension) that he is its firmest
stay.   He desires that Egypt and Syria may
be conceded to him and to his family in
hereditary descent.   He is ready to give up
Candia and Arabia when required to do so
by the Porte, and to pay to the latter a much
more considerable tribute than she has ever
hitherto received from those countries.
But, with regard to Candia, it must be
recollected, that that island contains a
Greek population, contented under the rule
of the Pacha, which will never again submit
to the dominion of the Porte; and as for
Arabia and the Holy Cities, who can protect
them, but the possessor of Egypt, from which
country they receive all their supplies; or
rather, from whence the army necessary for
the occupation of the country can alone be
fed ?

To whom, then, does the eye of the spectator naturally turn, on visiting the countries of the East, but to Mehemet Ali, who alone seems to be able, by his prominent position, to protect and preserve, if such a thing be possible, the integrity of the Ottoman empire? he has in his favour similarity of race and religion; he has power, resources, talents, and energy; he has had various and signal success in almost all his undertakings. Mehemet Ali seems the only Mussulman whose mind is of that superior cast to qualify him to estimate at its real value the civilization of his epoch, while he has done nothing to alienate or disgust the prejudices of his race. Does he not then seem the fittest, the only instrument, indeed, that can be brought forward to give strength, unity, and confidence to the Ottoman empire, and to protect her from the perfidious embraces of her powerful neighbour?

It is certainly curious to look back on

our policy, and to contemplate the present strength, progress, and resources of a man we now almost refuse to treat with—a man, too, with whom we have already negotiated as a sovereign ; for, in humble imitation of the Porte, who granted a constitution to the island of Samos, an island entirely inhabited by Greeks, and governed by a Greek prince, our authorities applied to Mehemet Ali to induce him to grant a similar one to Candia ; thereby, one would have supposed, re-cognising him as its legal possessor and sovereign.

We have also lately given a higher diplo-matic character to our Consul-General in Egypt than has been heretofore usual. We have taken the lead in this business, and have not been followed in it by any other power. This certainly appears somewhat contradictory, and recals to mind the shab-biness of Lord Liverpool's government, that refused to allow to Napoleon any other title than that of General, (one, to be sure, that was in fact his highest honour,) although it had negotiated with him as Emperor of the French.

The two fleets are arrayed in the port of Alexandria ; they are in good order, and the Turkish crews are now, it was believed, reconciled to the circumstances that had led to their junction with the others. They are nearly forty sail of first-rates, and sixty sail of all classes.

The Pacha has given himself up to the care and personal inspection of the fleet. He goes on board one or other of the ships every day, and has the men manœuvred in his presence. He has neglected no means of conciliation towards the Turkish portion of the fleet; and the writer was told, that he had had complete success. He gives the Capitan Pacha 4000l. a-year, and pays the other officers in proportion. The fleet is paid monthly ; and it is asserted, by official persons, that the Pacha does not owe one hundred thousand dollars, and that he has the whole of one year's crop of cotton and grain to dispose of.

It cannot be denied that his government is unpopular amongst the lower classes ; but the discontent is principally caused by the arbitrary and harassing manner in which the conscription is levied—a serious evil, that might, and ought to be, remedied, for numerous recruits are required, to maintain the efficiency of the large armies his present precarious position forces him to keep up.

The army in Syria amounts to nearly 90,000 men, including 20,000 irregulars ; that of Arabia to 40,000 men ; the one in Egypt to 15,000. St. Jean d'Acre has been lately restored, under the inspection of Soliman Pacha, (the French Colonel Selves,) and sixty new guns, with abundance of stores and ammunition, have been collected there. 35,000 men man his fleets, and four new eighty-gun ships have been recently laid on the stocks.

As regard the Pacha's financial, commercial, and agricultural exactions, however contrary they may seem to justice and wisdom, and opposed to the true principles of political economy, it is apprehended that the nature of his position in this respect is not generally understood. As successor to the property of the Mamelukes, he is the owner of three-fifths of the Delta and cultivated parts of Egypt; without his aid, authority, and discipline, the Fellahs would scarcely of themselves profit by the marvellous fertility of this district. He furnishes them with grain. He keeps open and makes new canals. He makes and keeps in repair the water-wheels necessary for the irrigation of the land; and, in return, he insists upon having the crop produced at a fixed price, on which he undoubtedly derives a considerable profit.

It is to his wisdom and vigour that the
British particularly owe the profits arising
from a considerable trade with the interior
of Syria, by Beyrout, Damascus, Scanda-
roon, and Aleppo. Before his rule, commerce did not exist there ; but he subdued
the Bedouin Arabs, made them submit to
his authority, and the result is a considerable commerce, which is yearly increasing,
and in which the English, among foreigners, are the principal gainers. In
addition to this extension of commerce,
European merchants derive the further
advantage, that, in the territories ruled by
Mehemet Ali, the duties on imports and
exports are fixed, and suffer no vexatious
or extortionary vacillation.

The original fixed duty of 3 per cent.,
which, under the arbitrary sway of the
Pachas sent from Constantinople, was forced
up to from 16 to 30 per cent., has been by
Mehemet re-established ; and it was not

supposed that the Commercial Treaty, of August, 1838, whatever may be the ultimate fate of Syria, could in any of its articles be brought into action. It is thought that this Treaty, of which so much has been said, and on which so many brilliant prospects for the commerce of these regions have been founded, will remain, as it has hitherto done, a dead letter.

Nor is there any fear, as some imagine, that, in the event of the death of Mehemet Ali, his eldest son, Ibrahim Pacha, would be found wanting. Marshal Marmont tells us, that he has considerable military talents; and it is well known that he has a remarkable aptitude for accounts and business, and that, were he sovereign, many of the manufacturing and other speculations of the father would be discontinued. It is but fair to add, that if there be any truth in what is asserted, respecting his devotion to the pleasures of the table, at least they have never been allowed to interfere with, or impede, the transaction of public business.

The territories of the Pacha are generally in a more flourishing condition than they have been in of late years, and they present a far better picture of cultivation than any other portion of the Ottoman dominions. The government of the Pacha is notoriously less obnoxious than that of the Porte to those under its dominion who do not profess the Mahomedan religion; in proof of which may be brought forward the fact, that a certain number of Jews who had expatriated themselves have returned to the Holy Land, and the one before stated, relating to the present contented state of the population of Candia.

The Pacha is a most polite and engaging old gentleman, easy of access, simple in manner, and unincumbered by state. He declares openly, that he knows he cannot resist if nations combine against him, or even cope with England; but he says, he is now an old man, has done the State some service, has not had altogether an obscure career, and if he is to fall he will do so honourably, and with arms in his hands.

He will do nothing against British interest, or individuals, until forced to act in self-defence; but once compelled to take a part, he will do so with vigour. He says he can, and will, raise the standard of his race in Asia Minor and the Turkish European Provinces; that he will foment a religious war, from one end of the Ottoman dominions to the other; that the inhabitants will respond to his call; and that he is not without friends, even at Constantinople.

The writer certainly heard, when there, that the old Mussulmen looked upon the Pacha as the only man who, in their degenerate days, had asserted and held up the ancient vigour and courage of their race.

No one can now visit Turkey without feeling that the existence of the Ottoman empire, if not at an end, at least, hangs on a thread; and it is surmised, that, ardent as Lord Ponsonby may be in its cause, and however much he may indulge in the hope that regeneration and strength will be brought about by peace, reform, and economy, he does not anticipate anything more than a temporary preservation of the integrity of the empire.

But, supposing the wishes of the allied powers complied with, who is to govern Syria? How is it to be governed? The feeble sway of the Turks, the return of the enervated, rapacious, interested, and extortionary rule of three or four favourites from Stamboul, will not be able to keep in check its turbulent and excited people. Anarchy will be the consequence; Russia will then naturally step in; and no one can now travel in that country without hearing of, and witnessing, the exertions she is making to secure for herself a footing and influence there.

Pilgrimages to the Holy Sepulchre are encouraged to a vast extent. At Easter, Russians, and other Greeks, flock there by thousands; and at no period of the year is there at Jerusalem less than from 200 to 300 of these devotees; whilst the town itself has as many as 5,000 permanent residents of that religion, out of 15,000, the gross amount of the inhabitants of the Holy City. Nothing is left undone to excite the people to the contemplation of the power and predominance of Russia.

Wherever you go, whether it be to the Holy Sepulchre, or to any of the places marked out by tradition or superstition, as having been the scene of some miracle or interesting fact connected with the history of our Saviour or the Virgin, there the magnificence and munificence of Russia is made

manifest by the display of some costly ornament or candelabra sent by the emperor :
and a gate in the Old Wall, now closed, is
pointed out as the one through which the
Greeks, with the Grand Duke Michael at
their head, are to make their entrance into
the Holy City, when it shall be delivered
out of the hands of the Infidels.   The writer
found many parts of Syria in a state of
partial insurrection, and many villages
abandoned by their inhabitants, who had
taken this step, it was said, to avoid the
conscription, and in the absence of the army,
which is concentrated on the Turkish frontier.

The writer has reason to think that the
Pacha knows that he is in great need of us ;
and we ought to feel that we stand in some
need of him and his influence.   We want
him to facilitate our intercourse across his
country with India, either by the Red Sea or
the Euphrates ; to make either or both secure and permanent.

Our object ought to be to make him power-ful; and at the same time that we prosecute our project of bolstering up the Turkish empire, to make him minister to our wants and interests in Syria and Egypt.

The Pacha knows that, however numerous his fleet, it dares not meet ours at sea; and he does not forget that we could blockade his ports and burn his ships, and could intercept his communication with his army at Adana and on the Taurus. He is not ignorant that one sloop of war would be sufficient to put an entire stop to all commu-nication between Arabia and Egypt, and at once annihilate his commerce, and force his army in that quarter to retreat, his supplies being thus cut off.

The fortress of Aden, at the entrance of the Red Sea, on which we have taken up a military position, and which is an important port for our steam navigation with Bombay, *ought never to be given up*, and ought to be so fortified, and so well garrisoned, as to place it out of the limit of possibility that any force the Arabians could bring against it could subdue it. These facts ought, therefore, to convince the Pacha and ourselves, that our interests are bound up together; and, so far as he is concerned, one must admit that there is no proof he does not give us of his disposition to serve us by facilitating the transit of goods and passengers from Alexandria to Suez.

Why then are we, of all people on earth, to quarrel with him? Why are we thus to play the game of Russia, and run the chance of exciting a civil war, that will not fail to open the door for her, and afford her a plea for intervention?

The Russians are very naturally pursuing their own objects; the French are equally at work to forward theirs in the Mediterranean, and attack our commerce everywhere; while we stand looking on in apparent oblivion, that the question is not one of merely European interest to us, but one vitally affecting our Indian possessions. We appear to be unmindful of this part of the question, and are allowing difficulties to be got up for us in all parts of our Asiatic possessions. Witness the late events in Persia—the necessity for the Affghanistan expedition—the intrigues which have given us so much annoyance from the Napaulese, on our north-eastern frontier—the preparations for attack got up in the heart of our most peaceable districts—at Kurnoul, midway between Madras and Hyderabad, where a depôt of upwards of 400 cannon and numerous fire-arms, which had been manufactured or collected there, was discovered. The insurrection at Sattara, in the immediate neighbourhood of Bombay and Poonah, which place we were compelled to subdue by force of arms. Witness the intrigues that are exciting the Burmese against us—

the Chinese break out—and all this within the space of two years, and almost simultaneously !

Who then can help surmising that these inconveniences are brought about by intrigues having the same object, though perhaps not fostered by a combined movement—and which extend to India on the one side, from Petersburg through Persia ; and on the other, through the East India colonies, which we, in 1815, were weak enough to leave in French hands ; and papers were found in possession of the Rajah of Sattara, which prove that he was instigated to revolt by the Portuguese government at Goa.

The writer cannot believe the reports he has read in the papers of the objects of Monsieur Brunow's mission ; but, if it be true that it has been proposed that the Russians shall occupy Asia Minor and Syria, with her armies, whilst we shall be allowed to have eight sail of the line in the Sea of

Marmora, and the tub thrown out to us of possession of the island of Candia, the result will be, the realization of all objects of Russian ambition, and probably war between France and ourselves ; for the French cannot but be made jealous by any project which has for its end the giving possession to us of that fertile island and eminently important military post.

The writer is well aware that the island of Candia is fertile and magnificent, that the great harbour on its north side offers every accommodation for a large fleet, and that it is defended by works thrown up (by the Venetians) for its protection ; but it seems to him that, however desirable such a conquest might be in many points of view, it ought to be a principal object with us to protect our Indian interests ; and that we might effectually do so with the aid of Mehemet Ali, without exciting the jealousy of any other power, or incurring the chances of war.

Indeed, he thinks it may be shewn that
we might be so successful in carrying out
this project, that our communications with
India through Egypt, which are hourly
increasing and becoming more important to
us, might, in the event of Mehemet Ali's
death, or in the failure of his progeny, or of
there being none of it fit to rule that country, throw the possession of it into our
hands, by so gradual a change, and so natural a course of events, as scarcely to excite the alarm or ill-will of any one. It ought
to be, however, our task to make Egypt
profitable and available to us *without* occupancy; and so to link the fortunes and
interests of Mehemet Ali and his descendants with our own, as to place him in a
state of real subjection to us, from which
neither he nor they would be able to escape.

Events are even now of themselves taking
this turn; already the Arabs on the line of
the Desert have been brought to understand

and appreciate the advantages to be derived from a dependence on our honour and good faith. The East India Company is served by the camel-owners cheaper than the Pacha himself; they receive promissory notes, payable at the British Consul's, for their contracts, the value of which they sometimes allow to remain for months in his hands.

In all disputes between natives and British, the former resort to the British Consul for justice, and are satisfied with his decision, without appeal; whereas, if a native has a dispute with one of any other nation, he generally refers the matter to the governor.

All, then, that we further need is, to encourage, protect, and make a friend of Mehemet Ali. The writer was assured, when in Egypt, that the people in the upper country and in Abyssinia, are anxious to get into intercourse with us, and that they have by them considerable quantities of gold-dust and ivory, which they would prefer disposing of to our merchants on the Red Sea, to allowing these objects of commerce to pass through the ordeal of the Pacha's custom-houses.

The campaign in Affghanistan having, by its effects, established our influence as far as Herat, would it not be politic in us to place Mehemet Ali *à cheval* on the Euphrates ?— perhaps to give him the occupancy of Bagdad, and thus secure for ourselves two peaceable communications with India, which can alone be effected through the aid of the Pacha.

He has been the first and the most successful in discovering the secret of keeping the Arabs in order, and we might always rely upon his efficacious and systematic support, for the best of all reasons, because his alliance with us would at once give him security for the future against all other powers, and would increase, if not double, his wealth and resources. On the other hand, he would well understand our power to paralyze his government were he refractory ; and our influence might be beneficially exerted to ameliorate the condition, and increase the comfort and happiness of the interesting people the Pacha and his descendants seem destined to govern.

APPENDIX II.

THE TALMUD.

(See vol. i. p. 317.)

It has been very generally believed among the Jews, that when God gave to Moses the written law, He gave him also another, not written; and that this was preserved by tradition among the doctors of the synagogue, until rabbi Judah, surnamed the Holy, collected these traditions together, and (150 B. c.) reduced them to writing. The collection thus formed received the name of Mishna, or Second Law. After a while, commentaries were written on the Mishna, and amongst these, that of rabbi

Johanas, composed about 230 A. D., and bearing the name of Gemara, or Completion, was the most celebrated. The Mishna and the Gemara together, form what is called the Jerusalem Talmud, or Doctrine; for, after the Jews had removed in great numbers to Babylon, the rabbis there composed new commentaries on the Mishna, and those, which were completed about 500 A. D., received the name of the Babylonian Talmud.

Fordington Vicarage,
   April 20, 1841.

APPENDIX III.

COMING OF THE MESSIAH.

(See vol. i. p. 318.)

Laurel Lodge, near Barnet,
January 14th, 1841.

MY DEAR SIR,—The ground of expectation now so prevalent among my poor brethren concerning the Messiah, rests on the authority of the ancient rabbins, more especially in an ancient Talmudical book, called *Zohar.*

But the fact is, that the rabbins themselves differ on this point, for, according to some, he must have appeared long ago;

and there is no *stronger* authority in the
Talmud why He should come *now*, than
there is that He should have come *previously*, according to the calculation of other
rabbins.

But then, the question is, Why do the
Jews so universally hang to *this* particular
period, seeing that they did not do so *previously?* My answer is, that it is not so
much the prediction of the rabbins, as it is
the change which the minds of that nation
have undergone of late years, that make
them now so sanguine concerning a decision
on this all-important head.

For years past my poor nation (by whatever means, my limits will not allow me to
enter upon) have become restless on this
point. They applied to their rabbins, and
these pointed to this period; as a year passed
away, that restless spirit increased, and at
no period, since the days of the apostles, I
believe, have my brethren manifested such

a concern for the fulfilment of Jehovah's promise, as at this period.

The truth is, my nation are half convinced that they have no foundation for their hopes, and, like a man who is spurred on by hope and fear, they long for the decisive event.

Speaking scripturally, we are living in the last days. But even without scripture testimony, it is quite clear to me, that my nation, who have now, for 1800 years, remained *unaltered*, cannot possibly continue *so* another century. Should even the change progress at no greater rate among them than what it did the last twenty years, what a result must that lead to in forty or fifty years !

I fear, my dear Sir, that you will scarcely be able to read my German-English note. Excuse this haste; I have just returned from a journey, and my hands are full. I shall be happy to furnish you with any information I am able. Our Bible class, I am happy to say, does well. That the God of Abraham, Isaac, and Jacob, may bless you with the blessing of Abraham, is,

My dear Sir,

The prayer of yours faithfully,

For Jesus' sake,

A. M. MYERS.

To the Hon. William Cowper.

APPENDIX IV.

_____

RETURN OF THE JEWS TO THE HOLY LAND.

(See vol. i. p. 318.)

THE following curious communication has recently appeared in a Jersey paper :

"TO THE EDITOR OF THE BRITISH PRESS.

" SIR,—For the information of such of your readers as sympathize with the Jews in their present dispersion, and who desire their restoration to the land of their fathers, I herewith send you extracts from a German newspaper, which ' betoken a movement among the continental Jews in relation to

the late crisis in Syria,' as the editor remarks :—

" ' We have a country, the inheritance of
our fathers, finer, more fruitful, better situate for commerce, than many of the most
celebrated portions of the globe. Environed
by the deep-delled Taurus, the lively shores
of the Euphrates, the lofty steppes of Arabia,
and of rocky Sinai, our country extends
along the shores of the Mediterranean,
crowned by the towering cedars of Lebanon,
the source of a hundred rivulets and brooks,
which spread fruitfulness over shady dales,
and confer wealth on the contented inhabitants. A glorious land! situate at the far-
thest extremity of the sea which connects
three-quarters of the globe, over which the
Phœnicians, our brethren, sent their numerous fleets to the shores of Albion and the
rich coasts of Lithuania, near both to the
Red Sea and the Persian Gulf; the perpetual
sources of the traffic of the world, on the

way from Persia and India, to the Caspian and Black Sea, the central country of the commerce between the East and the West.

" 'Every country has its peculiarity; every people their own nature. Syria, with its extensive surrounding plains unfavourable to regular cultivation, is a land of transit, of communication, of caravans. No people on the earth have lived so true to their calling from the first as we have done. We are a trading people, born for the country where little food is necessary, and this is furnished by nature almost spontaneously to the temperate inhabitants, but not for the heavy soils of the ruder north.

" 'In no country of the earth are our brethren so numerous as in Syria; in none do they live in as dense masses; so independent of the surrounding inhabitants; in none do they persevere so steadfastly in their faith in the promise of the fathers, as on the beautiful shores of the Orontes. In Damascus alone live near 60,000.

" ' The Arab has maintained his language and his original country ; on the Nile, in the deserts, as far as Sinai, and beyond the Jordan, he feeds his flocks. In the elevated plains of Asia Minor the Turkoman has conquered for himself a second country, the birthplace of the Osman ; but Syria and Palestine are depopulated. For centuries the battle-field between the sons of Alla and of the Arabian wilderness, the inhabitants of the West and the half-nomadic Persians, none have been able to establish themselves and maintain their nationality ; no nation can claim the name of Syrian. A chaotic mixture of all the tribes and tongues, remnants of migrations from the north and south, they disturb one another in the possession of the glorious land where our fathers for so many centuries emptied the cup of joy and woe, where every clod is drenched

with the blood of our heroes when their bo-
dies were buried under the ruins of Jerusalem.

" 'The power of our enemies is gone, the
angel of discord has long since mown down
their mighty host, and yet ye do not bestir
yourselves, people of Jehovah! What hin-
ders? Nothing but your own supineness.

" 'Think you that Mehemet Ali or the
Sultan in Stamboul will not be convinced
that it would be better for him to be the
protector of a peaceful and wealthy people,
than with infinite loss of men and money to
contend against the ever-repeated, mutually
provoked insurrections of the Turks and
Arabs, of whom neither the one nor the
other are able to give prosperity to the
country?

" 'Our probation was long, in all countries, from the North Pole to the South.
There is no trade, no art, which we have not

practised, no science in which we cannot shew splendid examples. Where will you find better proclaimers of civilisation to the wild tribes of the east ?

" 'People of Jehovah ! raise yourselves from your thousand years' slumber ! Rally round leaders ; have really the will ; a Moses will not be wanting. The rights of nations will never grow old ; take possession of the land of your fathers ; build a third time the temple of Zion, greater and more magnificent than ever. Trust in the Lord, who has led you safely through the vale of misery thousands of years. He also will not forsake you in your last conflict.'

" These extracts shew that the Jews are exhorting one another to return to, and take possession of their father-land, now that their God is ' drying up the waters of the great river Euphrates,' to ' prepare a way' for them, by the combined forces of Turkey acting against the Egyptians, as predicted in Daniel, xi. 40—43,* Rev. xvi. 12.

" For this is the year ordained of God for reinstating the descendants of Abraham, Isaac, and Jacob, in their own land, no more to be dispossessed of it by the Gentiles. (Jer. xvi. 14, 15.) And, when returning, God will give them the tabernacle, and the ark, and the altar of incense, which he commanded Jeremiah to hide in a hollow cave in Mount Nebo, when their ancestors were going into captivity in Babylon. For ' then the Lord shall shew them these things, and the glory of the Lord shall appear, and the cloud also, as it was shewn unto Moses, and as when Solomon desired that the place might be honourably sanctified.' — See 2 Mac. ii. 1—8.

" From the subjoined calculation, drawn

* Turkey is there called " the King of the North," and Egypt " the King of the South," because those countries are north and south of the Jews' country.

from scriptural data, it is obviously proved that the year 1840 terminated the ' 2,300 days' or years, ordained by God for giving the Jews over to the Gentiles, by them to ' be trodden under foot for their transgression of the daily sacrifice.'—(Dan. viii. 13, 14 ; Luke, xxi. 20—24.)   We may therefore expect the Jews to ' be received unto mercy,' in their own land, this present year 1841, and to commence rebuilding their cities and the temple as in former years, as predicted in Jer. xxxi. 31—40 ; Ez. xxxvi. 24—38 ; xxxvii. ; and as spoken of by themselves in the extracts I send you.   And ' then shall the sanctuary be cleansed,' as predicted in Dan. viii. 14, (some say in 1843.)

" According to Dan. ix. 24, those 2,300 days, or years, began 70 weeks, or 490 years, before the death and resurrection of Christ   ...   .   490 years.

" From these 490 years, deduct the natural life of Christ   ...   .   34 years.

" And it proves, that those 2,300 days,
  or years, began, B.C.... ... ...   456 years.
" To these 456 years, add 1,840 years,
  and 4 years for the error of the vulgar
  era, in all 1,844 years   ... . 1,844 years.
  ———————

" And you have the number of the days,
  or years of the vision... ... ... 2,300 years.

" This subject receives additional force
and interest from the following extract from
a Liverpool publication of December last :
' With such anxiety are the Jews regarded
by the different Cabinets of Europe, that it
is upon this issue, Who shall possess the
land which God gave to their forefathers ?
that the question of peace or war now de-
pends, and their return to Palestine, under
the guarantee of the Allied Powers, has
been suggested as the most effectual mode
of preserving peace among the nations.
' The dry bones' are beginning to shake,
and appearances bring the words of the
Psalmist to our minds : ' Thou shalt arise

and have mercy upon Zion, for the time to favour her, yea, the set time is come, for thy servants take pleasure in her stones, and favour the dust thereof.'

" If these observations be found to accord with Divine Revelation, the present position of the Jews not only presents a most interesting object for contemplation, but must also lead every serious inquirer to admire the watchfulness of Jehovah over this ancient people during the lapse of so many ages, and at the same time to awaken the attention of professing Christians to the great events that must yet precede, and shall follow, their restoration to the land of their fathers, recorded in Ez. xxxvi., xxxvii., xxxviii., xxxix.; Luke, xxi. 24—28; Romans, xi.   " Yours, &c.

                    " PHILIP BOLTON.

" *St. Helier's, Jan.* 20, 1841."

THE END.

T. C. Savill, Printer, 107, St. Martin's Lane.

www.ingramcontent.com/pod-product-compliance
Lightning Source LLC
Chambersburg PA
CBHW080819020726
47501CB00009B/2346